Crown and parliaments, 1558–1689

Graham E. Seel

The Manchester Grammar School

David L. Smith

Selwyn College, Cambridge

CAMBRIDGE
UNIVERSITY PRESS

For our parents, with love and gratitude

CAMBRIDGE UNIVERSITY PRESS
Cambridge, New York, Melbourne, Madrid, Cape Town, Singapore, São Paulo

Cambridge University Press
The Edinburgh Building, Cambridge CB2 8RU, UK

www.cambridge.org
Information on this title: www.cambridge.org/9780521775373

First published 2001

A catalogue record for this publication is available from the British Library

ISBN 978-0-521-77537-3 paperback

Transferred to digital printing 2008

Text design by Newton Harris Design Partnership

ACKNOWLEDGEMENTS
Fotomas Index (UK), pp. 4, 45, 95; Mary Evans Picture Library, p. 77; Public Record
Office, pp. 12, 64.

The cover illustration is of *Charles I in Three Positions* (1600–49), a painting after
Van Dyck by Carlo Maratta or Maratti (1625–1713). Reproduced by courtesy of the
Trustees of the Weston Park Foundation UK/Bridgeman Art Library.

Contents

Contents

Introduction

The title of this book may risk seeming slightly old-fashioned at the beginning of the twenty-first century. In particular, to focus on the relationship between crown and parliament might be thought to have connotations of the 'Whig' interpretation, which saw English history as a long progression towards the modern constitutional monarchy. In Whig eyes, English history involved a prolonged series of conflicts between royal ambitions and popular liberties, stoutly defended by parliament. Gradually the tyrannical ambitions of various monarchs were thwarted and the forces of liberty and democracy triumphed. The monarchy became progressively more and more limited in its powers.

Within this interpretation, no period possessed more decisive importance than the late sixteenth and seventeenth centuries. The Stuart period saw two revolutions, the first extremely bloody, the second largely peaceful; one monarch was tried and publicly executed, another in effect deposed. To many historians this seemed the decisive stage at which royal ambitions to emulate continental absolutism were frustrated. In many Whig accounts this was a crucial watershed in English history. Elizabeth's difficulties with her parliaments were seen as a kind of preface to the conflicts of the following century, while the period from the early eighteenth century onwards was viewed as a journey down a path whose basic direction had already been set by the 1690s.

However, over the past two decades much of this interpretation has been vigorously challenged. The 'revisionist' historians, such as Geoffrey Elton, Conrad Russell and John Morrill, have argued that conflict was not inherent in the late Tudor or early Stuart state and suggested that this was in many ways a stable polity. They believe that it is anachronistic to read the English Civil Wars of the 1640s back into earlier decades, and that the Whig interpretation rests on an assumption that perceives events as moving towards a predetermined goal. Instead, they argue that we need to reconstruct the past on its own terms, to retrieve its political culture as authentically as possible, and not to ascribe significance to those features of the past that appear to prefigure our own world.

It is, nevertheless, possible to achieve a balance between these different views, one which fully acknowledges the important insights of 'revisionism' without losing sight of the fact that the late Tudor and Stuart periods were of immense significance in England's political, constitutional and religious history. After all, throughout these years political stability depended crucially on the way in which the monarch interacted with the privy council, the court and parliament; on the relationship between royal powers and the rule of law; and on the monarch's management of the church. These relationships and dynamics lay at the heart of the English polity and are vital in explaining both why it collapsed in the mid-seventeenth century, and how it was later reconstructed.

These relationships were not static, and these years saw changes of fundamental significance in them. In 1558, the queen could summon and dissolve parliament at will, could follow her own religious preferences and still remain queen whatever she chose, could raise taxation on royal authority without consulting parliament, could suspend parliamentary statutes, and could dismiss judges whenever she wished. By the 1700s much of this picture had changed. Parliament was now a permanent part of government; rather than meeting intermittently it had to meet at least every three years, and in practice it henceforth met every year. Parliament subsidised royal government with annual grants (the 'civil list'), and the monarch could no longer raise any money by their own authority. Parliament monitored the government's financial conduct, and ensured that its grants were used in the ways it intended. The monarch had to uphold statutes and could no longer suspend their operation. Judges had tenure for as long as they did good work, and could not be dismissed at the monarch's whim. The monarch was no longer free to choose their own religion; they had to be a communicant member of the Church of England – those who were not were debarred from the throne. In these and other important respects, constitutional safeguards had been developed to regulate royal action and guard against the idiosyncrasies of an individual monarch's personality.

This book traces how these changes came about. It examines the limits that were placed on royal powers, and the reasons why this was done. It looks at the role that the personalities of particular monarchs played in bringing about these developments. It takes the theme of the changing nature of royal powers and the limits upon them as a way of charting a path through the complex and turbulent events from the accession of Elizabeth I to that of William and Mary.

The first chapter analyses the position when Elizabeth came to the throne in 1558; while the final chapter adopts the same approach for 1689, when William and Mary were proclaimed king and queen, and the years immediately afterwards. These two chapters thus provide snapshots of the English polity at the beginning and end of the period. In between, the four central chapters examine the events that led from the first position to the second. These chapters consider in turn the periods 1558–1603, 1603–25, 1625–60 and 1660–88. At the end, there is a chart of key dates and also a bibliography suggesting ideas for further reading on this subject.

We hope that the significance of the period, and the changes that occurred during it, will emerge very clearly in the pages that follow, without returning to a 'Whiggish' interpretation or implying that this was the only way in which things could have developed. Indeed, one of the central themes of the book is the role of the contingent and the crucial importance of individual personalities in the unfolding of events. In a sense, this book charts a fascinating journey, the destination of which was unknown to those at the time, but which turned out to be very different from the starting-point.

The position in 1558

The monarchy: nature and powers

England in 1558 was a personal monarchy. The monarch was seen as the apex of the social order and of the political system. Government was royal government, conducted in the monarch's name, and all public offices in both central and local government were held on commissions from the monarch. The courts of law were likewise the monarch's courts, exercising justice on behalf of the monarch. The monarch was the embodiment of the body politic, and the monarch's personality necessarily had an immense influence on political priorities and decisions. As David Loades has written, 'the monarch was the keystone in the arch of government: the shaper of policy and the maker of decisions'.[1]

The powers that the monarch wielded were very extensive but not unlimited, and were known collectively as the royal 'prerogative'. These powers were usually divided into two branches, the ordinary and the absolute. The ordinary prerogative powers were 'defined in the law of the realm', and included powers such as the right to appoint to public office, to dispense justice and to regulate trade. These powers were determined and limited by the law. The absolute prerogative powers were not so defined, and applied to emergency situations such as the making of peace and war, or the taking of necessary action to preserve national security. These were discretionary powers that ran alongside the law; they were not constrained by it, but equally they could not contravene it. This enabled contemporaries to describe royal powers – in terms which to modern ears sound like a contradiction in terms – as 'absolute and legally limited'. The main problem with this concept was that the boundary between the absolute and ordinary prerogatives was not clearly defined, and political stability depended to a crucial extent on monarchs establishing an effective working relationship with their leading subjects. In practice, this was not always easy to achieve in a system that depended so much upon the interaction of individual personalities.

The public image and iconography of the monarch were carefully cultivated to reinforce the perception of the monarch as God's chosen ruler. In an age before film or television, the mass of the population became familiar with the monarch's image primarily through coins, medallions or engravings. For a more elite audience, portraiture provided a means of propagating the likeness of the monarch and one that directly reflected the political culture of the period.

The 'Rainbow Portrait' of Elizabeth I, from the original at Hatfield House, drawn by William Derby and engraved by T. A. Dean c.1825.

One notable example of the latter is the 'Rainbow Portrait' at Hatfield House in which Elizabeth's costume is depicted as covered with eyes and ears to symbolise her knowledge, insight and all-embracing awareness of her kingdom. She holds a rainbow as a symbol of peace. In this, as in many other portraits of the queen, the monarch's power and wisdom as well as her role as God's lieutenant on earth are powerfully affirmed.

The queen's court reinforced the symbolism of monarchy by providing a splendid setting in which the monarch lived from day to day. In a sense, the court did not have a fixed location but followed the monarch wherever she went. Elizabeth was famous for her regular summer progresses, when she and her courtiers travelled round selected parts of her kingdom, staying with particular subjects who were both deeply flattered and often secretly appalled at the expense that was involved. But the court was not only a lavish setting for the monarch; it also fulfilled a vital political function as a point of contact between the monarch and some of her leading subjects. Those who held senior court offices, or who visited court regularly, often had direct personal access to the queen that could give them a degree of political influence denied to those away from court (as the earl of Essex was to discover, to his cost, in the 1590s). The court was a vital channel through which the monarch could be informed of developments in the realm at large, and kept abreast of changing currents of opinion within the political elite. Until the 1590s, Elizabeth proved remarkably adept at balancing different groups and individuals, and generally avoided leaving people feeling marginalised.[2]

Part of that success lay in Elizabeth's realisation that royal government depended to a crucial extent on the co-operation of the political elite. At both national and local levels, the crown relied on members of the nobility and gentry to implement policy and to conduct administration; without their active support, the Tudor state entirely lacked the bureaucratic machinery to enforce its will. Elizabeth soon learned the vital lesson that although the crown wielded very extensive powers, and was surrounded with all the trappings and symbolism of authority, its powers were actually greatest when exercised in collaboration with the political elite. As the following sections will show, that was a central feature of Tudor government that monarchs ignored at their peril. This was the profound truth which Henry VIII acknowledged when he told members of parliament in 1542: 'We at no time stand so highly in our estate royal as in the time of Parliament, wherein we as head and you as members are conjoined and knit together into one body politic.'[3] The full force of this remark becomes clear when we turn to examine the role of parliament and its relationship with the crown in this period.

The role of parliaments

The historiography of Tudor, and especially Elizabethan, parliaments was for a long time coloured by reading the Civil War between crown and parliament in the 1640s back into the previous century. Only over the past 20 years, through the work of 'revisionists' such as Michael Graves and Geoffrey Elton, has it been fully recognised that crown and parliament should not be seen as natural antagonists, already limbering up for the conflict of the mid-seventeenth century. Instead, it is important to remember that parliament was an instrument of royal government, not a counterweight to it. It existed to make the monarch's rule more effective, not less. Ever since its earliest origins in the thirteenth century, parliament had existed as an agency of the crown, and the monarch could summon, prorogue or dissolve it at will. The monarch could thus choose when, and for how long, parliament met.[4]

However, although monarchs controlled when parliament sat, the powers that they exercised jointly with parliament were greater than those which they wielded on their own. From the 1530s onwards it was universally recognised that acts of parliament (statutes) were the highest form of law in England. In order to be valid, statutes had to receive the assent of both houses of parliament (the Lords and the Commons) and of the monarch. There was no limit to the powers of statutes, and no way of undoing them except by another statute. The crown could, however, suspend the operation of a statute temporarily, or dispense (exempt) particular individuals from the force of a statute. As a last resort, monarchs could also refuse to give their assent to bills that had passed both houses of parliament by using the royal veto.[5] But such powers were used very sparingly, and in practice the monarch's unilateral powers palled in comparison with those exercised in conjunction with parliament. Monarchs could issue proclamations on their own authority, but these could not touch life or limb or infringe common law rights of property. By contrast, statutes could enact a death sentence without a common law trial (by act of attainder). It was during the Reformation Parliament (1529–36) that the omnicompetence of statute was demonstrated more clearly than ever before. In these years statutes were used to enact measures as varied and momentous as the break with Rome, a fundamental refashioning of the nation's religious life, a redefining of the law of treason and a rearrangement of the line of succession. When working with their parliaments there was almost nothing that Tudor monarchs could not do. The queen acting alone was thus less powerful than the 'Queen-in-Parliament', and the latter possessed a range of powers and a freedom of action well beyond those of most continental rulers in this period.

As well as passing legislation, there were other functions that added to parliament's usefulness to the crown. From the fourteenth century onwards the Commons had established its right to assent to certain categories of taxation, of which the most significant were called the subsidy and the fifteenth and tenth. It was generally assumed that these formed part of the crown's 'extraordinary' revenues, only granted in times of 'evident and urgent' need, such as wartime or other national emergency. At other times, it was expected that the crown would live off its 'ordinary' revenues, which comprised principally income from crown lands, customs duties, feudal revenues (especially wardship and purveyance) and the profits of justice (mainly fines and fees from the law courts). The Commons could refuse the monarch's requests for 'extraordinary' supply, and this 'power of the purse' gave the house the potential to exert political leverage, demanding concessions as the price for granting revenue. Yet parliaments were relatively restrained in their use of this power. Elizabeth requested supply in all but one (1572) of her 13 parliamentary sessions, and each time these requests were granted. The only instance of any resistance in the Commons was in 1593 when the Lords seemed in danger of pre-empting the Commons' right to initiate taxation.[6] Grants of extraordinary revenue were among the facilities that made parliaments most directly useful to monarchs, and the latter would not have continued to call them as often as they did had they not anticipated a reasonable likelihood of gaining the supply they wanted. Indeed, the need for such a grant of taxation was often among the most immediate reasons why a monarch decided to summon parliament.

There were also other motives. Parliament acted as the monarch's 'Great Council', and this term was frequently used as a synonym for parliament throughout this period. Unlike the inner, privy council, which generally met weekly, parliament met intermittently – only 13 times during Elizabeth's 45-year reign, lasting a total of around 145 weeks (approximately 34 months). Elizabeth liked to keep parliamentary sessions fairly short, and the average length of session during her reign was about 11 weeks.[7] Parliament was thus, in Conrad Russell's memorable phrase, 'an event and not an institution'.[8] However, parliament had the great advantage of bringing monarchs and their advisers into direct contact with leading members of the political elite: the nobility (lords temporal) and the bishops (lords spiritual) in the Lords, and the representatives of the counties and boroughs (who were predominantly gentry) in the Commons. This made parliament another invaluable point of contact between monarch and subjects. According to the writs summoning them to parliament, members were required to advise the monarch on 'urgent and arduous affairs', and such counsel was crucial in making those at the heart of government aware of trends and opinions in the nation at large.

Yet there was also the potential for tension and disagreement. What happened if parliament offered advice that the monarch had not asked for or did not wish to hear? Was parliament's role in advising the monarch a duty or a right? Were there certain matters on which parliament could not presume to advise? There were no agreed answers to these questions, and we shall see that they generated regular disputes between successive monarchs and their parliaments.

Another key function of parliaments was to exercise justice on the monarch's behalf. Contemporaries often referred to the 'High Court of Parliament', and this was a further way in which parliament operated as an agency of royal government. The House of Lords acted as a court of appeal, a function that fell into disuse during the sixteenth century but was dramatically revived from 1621 onwards. It could hear cases referred to it from one of the central law courts. The Commons could not act independently as a court of law in the same way, but the two houses could work together, for example in the process known as impeachment – in which the Commons acted as prosecutors and the Lords as judge and jurors. Such trials followed common law principles concerning the hearing of witnesses under oath. Impeachment had not been used since 1459 but was revived in 1621 and thereafter was regularly used until the early nineteenth century to punish unpopular royal advisers. This had the potential to cause conflict between the monarch and parliament if the former wished to protect an adviser whom the latter wished to impeach.

In order to fulfil these diverse functions as effectively as possible, parliament enjoyed various privileges and liberties. Members of the House of Lords had various privileges by virtue of their status as peers; these included freedom from arrest or legal suits while parliament was sitting, the right to sit in the Lords, and the right – if unavoidably absent – to appoint another peer as a proxy to vote on the peer's behalf. The House of Commons, on the other hand, had to petition the monarch to grant its privileges at the beginning of each new parliamentary session. The speaker (a crown nominee) would request that the monarch grant the house its four ancient liberties, and although this was largely a formality by the later sixteenth century it could not yet be taken completely for granted.

These liberties were fourfold: the right of access to the Lords and to the monarch, the right to correct calumnies of the house, liberty of speech and freedom from arrest or legal suits while parliament was sitting. The Commons jealously guarded these privileges and was extremely sensitive to any perceived encroachment on them. As we shall see, this was consistently a touchy area between monarchs and their parliaments throughout this period.

Equally, because so much has been made in the older literature of moments of conflict between crown and parliament, it needs stressing that parliament was an institution of royal government, not in any way a rival to it. The two houses were not divided, as today, into the government benches and those of the opposition. There was not an opposition in the modern sense; all members were there to serve and advise the monarch, and such groupings as did exist were generally fluid and transient in nature. Disagreements occurred over how best to advise the monarch, and above all over what to do if the monarch refused to listen to parliamentary advice. But this was all part of the workings of the monarch's 'Great Council' rather than a symptom of resistance to the crown. Very often, parliamentary criticism of royal policies reflected the spilling over of debates within the court and privy council into the Lords and Commons. Parliament in the mid-sixteenth century thus needs to be seen not so much as a limitation on the crown's powers as a part of an organic, interlocking system of government – what contemporaries called the 'body politic'. The monarch was the centre or head of the political system, and the conciliar institutions spread outwards from it in concentric circles. Parliament formed the outermost circle, and within it lay the inner circle, the privy council.

The privy council and royal advisers

The body known as the privy council had emerged in 1540 as part of Thomas Cromwell's reforms, and grew out of the large and relatively informal medieval king's council which had survived into the early Tudor period. The members of the privy council were personally selected by the monarch; nobody sat *ex officio* or as of right, although the membership normally included the two secretaries of state and such senior officers as the lord chancellor and the lord treasurer. The size and composition of the council lay very much within the monarch's discretion, and this complete freedom of appointment was not challenged until the 1640s. Like Henry VIII and Edward VI, but unlike Mary, Elizabeth preferred to keep her council small in number; it never had more than 20 members, and sometimes as few as 11.[9] This made for efficient government, which was essential given the immense range and volume of business that the council handled. Essentially, the council was the chief instrument of executive government. It met at least once a week (often more regularly), and the matters it discussed and the letters and orders it issued covered all aspects of government throughout the realm.[10]

If administration of every kind of state business was one of the council's key roles, a second lay in advising the monarch. As with the 'Great Council' of parliament, the ways in which the privy council counselled the monarch were not precisely defined; much depended on personal relationships and there was scope for considerable disagreement and tension. Many privy councillors felt that they had a duty to offer the queen advice, even if it was unpalatable to her. In 1566, when Elizabeth faced concerted pressure from her councillors to marry, the earl of Pembroke told her that they were 'only doing what was fitting for the good of the country, and advising her what was best for her, and if she did not think fit to adopt the advice, it was still their duty to offer it'.[11] In general, most Elizabethan privy councillors held the view that it was their duty to give the queen advice completely openly and honestly and then, once she had reached a decision, to implement her wishes, regardless of their private views. As the longest serving of Elizabeth's councillors, William Cecil, Lord Burghley, put it:

> As long as I may be allowed to give advice, I will not change my opinion by affirming the contrary, for that were to offend God, to whom I am sworn first; but as a servant I will obey her Majesty's commandment . . . [After] I have performed my duty as a counsellor, [I] shall in my heart wish her commandments such good success as I am sure she intends.[12]

Such loyal sentiments nevertheless left considerable scope in practice for manipulating the queen, for example by carefully selecting the information brought before her or by presenting arguments with a particular slant. Elizabeth of course realised that this went on, and once remarked that her councillors 'dealt with me like physicians who, ministering a drug, make it more acceptable by giving it a good aromatical savour, or when they give pills do gild them all over'.[13]

It was not easy for a monarch to guard against such manipulation, but one of the most effective ways was to ensure that as wide a range of viewpoints as possible was represented within the council. This was exactly what was needed to make it work efficiently as a conciliar body, and the Elizabethan council generally contained a variety of opinion that was remarkable in so small a body. Those figures who took a strongly Protestant line and urged military action against Spain, such as the earl of Leicester and Sir Francis Walsingham, were balanced by other more pragmatic and cautious figures – including Burghley, the earl of Sussex and Sir Christopher Hatton. The queen thus kept in touch with at least some of the different strands of opinion in the nation at large. Such a wide variety of views also enabled her to play her councillors off against each other. Very often, she preferred to conduct business informally, with small groups of councillors, outside the full council meetings. It was open to monarchs to receive advice from whoever they chose, including prominent individuals who were not actually members of the privy council; both Leicester and Essex, for example, enjoyed the queen's confidence for several years before being appointed to the council.

The third and final aspect of the council's functions was that, like parliament, it exercised a judicial role. The privy councillors, together with the two chief justices (of the Courts of King's Bench and Common Pleas), could sit as a law court known as the Court of Star Chamber. This court was presided over by the lord chancellor and usually met twice a week during the law terms. By the later sixteenth century it had established itself as a highly efficient court, very popular among litigants for its speed and perceived fairness of jurisdiction. The later dark connotations that surrounded its name and led to its abolition in 1641 stemmed from events during the 1630s and should not be allowed to cloud the positive impact of the court in earlier decades.

All in all, the privy council at its best could work as a highly versatile and effective institution. It stood at the very heart of government. As with parliament, it existed to inform and guide royal action rather than to restrict it; equally, again like parliament, the potential for friction existed if the monarch resented the advice that was offered or refused to accept it. As we shall see in the next chapter, in Elizabeth's reign this was especially true of issues such as whether the queen should marry, the succession, and the handling of the Catholic threat. On such matters the queen's characteristic reluctance to act drove some of her councillors to desperation, and disputes within court and council spilled over into parliament. But such tensions took place within a context of profound loyalty to the crown and stemmed from fears that the queen was acting irresponsibly and neglecting the nation's best interests, rather than from a wish to limit her powers as such. Much of the stability of the council rested on its capacity to represent a range of views among its members, and to avoid leaving prominent individuals feeling marginalised. For the greater part of her reign Elizabeth achieved this, and it was only in her final years that the balance became seriously upset, leading to the earl of Essex's abortive coup in 1601.

Law courts and the rule of law

We saw above that in mid-sixteenth-century England royal powers were regarded as both 'absolute' and 'legally limited'. One consequence of this idea was a similar paradox in the perceived relationship between the monarch and the rule of law. On the one hand, the monarch was conventionally regarded as the creator of the laws of England, and in the Coronation Oath they swore to 'confirm to the people of England the laws and customs granted by the Kings of England'. On the other hand, since the Middle Ages there had developed within England an important constitutional tradition that asserted that monarchs had to abide by the rule of law as much as their subjects and could not act arbitrarily. In the thirteenth century, the judge Henry de Bracton had formulated the maxim *debet rex esse sub lege* ('the king must be within the law'). This principle was further reinforced in the later fifteenth century by Chief Justice Sir John Fortescue, who described the English polity as *dominium politicum et regale*, meaning a form of government that was both 'political' and 'royal'. Within this, there were certain royal discretionary powers that were not defined by law, but that had to be exercised in ways which did not actually infringe the laws.

In theory this was a perfectly coherent doctrine. It was argued that the common law existed for the good of the commonwealth, and royal powers could only legitimately be exercised for the public good (*pro bono publico*), rather than for the monarch's own good (*pro bono suo*), which was a hallmark of tyranny; therefore there was logically no reason for the monarch's will and the law to come into conflict. Contemporary legal and political commentators regularly celebrated this almost mystical symbiosis between royal powers and the law. In theory, the authority of both was held to derive from divine right. That belief was reinforced by the fact that all courts were the monarch's courts in which legal officers, appointed by the crown, exercised justice in the monarch's name.

Tudor England knew no concept of the separation of powers between executive, legislature and judiciary. Just as the 'High Court' of parliament was an agency of royal government, so the monarch appointed the judges who sat in the central law courts.

These central law courts may be divided into three categories. Firstly, there were the three common law courts: King's Bench, Common Pleas and Exchequer. These courts operated the common law, that blend of custom and precedent which formed the basis of English criminal law and much civil law. Secondly, there were the courts which operated the system of law known as equity. These included the Court of Requests and above all Chancery. By the sixteenth century, equity had evolved into a distinct form of law, with its own system of rules and precedents. It grew out of the application of principles of natural justice, common sense and fairness to particular problems; it supplemented the common law and filled gaps where the latter had failed to adapt to changing circumstances. This in turn meant that although in theory the common law and equity complemented each other, the potential always existed for conflicts over jurisdiction; in particular, many common lawyers resented the interference of the equity courts in cases which they regarded as their business. Thirdly, there were the prerogative courts, of which the most important was the Star Chamber. This was the privy council sitting as a court of law (with the addition of the judges), and it was responsible for investigating public order offences and alleged perversions of justice. In all these courts, the judges were appointed and dismissed by the monarch, and they sat during the royal pleasure (*durante bene placito*); this gave the monarch considerable influence over the judiciary, but one that it would be highly unwise to exert too frequently and too forcefully.

A striking image that neatly symbolises the fact that the operation of the law courts was conducted in the monarch's name is the miniature depiction of the monarch at the head of a plea roll in the Court of Queen's Bench. From these premises also stemmed the axiom that the monarch can do no wrong. Given that no individuals can be tried in, or convicted by, their own courts, it was thought impossible for the monarch to commit any wrong known to the law. As one judge put it in 1562: 'The King cannot do any wrong, nor will his prerogative be any warrant to him to do an injury to another.'[14]

There was, nevertheless, a way in which a subject could challenge royal actions and seek redress, which was to submit a petition to the monarch. These petitions could be of two kinds. A petition of grace asked the monarch to do something that lay within their free choice, but to which the subject had no

Elizabeth I in majesty, an illuminated capital from a plea roll, Easter 1572.

existing right. A petition of right, by contrast, asserted that royal action had infringed a right that already existed in law, for example by violating a statute. These petitions could be submitted by an institution such as parliament or by private individuals, and they gave some reality to the claim that the monarch was subject to the law.

All these ideas sounded fine in theory; in practice, the relationship between the crown and the rule of law depended to a considerable extent on the monarch and those who practised the law respecting each other and being able to work together without believing that either was encroaching on the terrain of the other. This was very often a matter of personalities and perceptions. With care and sensitivity on both sides conflict could be avoided, but in the absence of such qualities there was no mechanism to reconcile them or arbitrate between them if this failed to occur naturally.

Royal authority and the rule of law were not inherently hostile to each other, and such a notion would have shocked those who lived in mid-Tudor England. However, the fundamental lack of definition in such a system meant that the potential for conflict always existed. The precise boundaries between royal powers and the law remained very vague. A further difficulty lay in the definition of an emergency. Everyone agreed that the monarch could wield certain discretionary powers in an emergency such as a war for the preservation of the realm. But it was unclear what happened if the monarchs used such powers outside an emergency, or whether their claim that an emergency existed could be challenged at law. These intractable issues lay half concealed during the reigns of Elizabeth I and James I, but they were to become a cause of bitter controversy under Charles I.

The Elizabethan church settlement

When Elizabeth became queen in November 1558, no aspect of government presented her with greater problems than the future of the church. Over the previous 25 years, Elizabeth's three predecessors had implemented a series of dramatic changes in the nation's religious life. Henry VIII had repudiated papal jurisdiction and established himself as supreme head of the church yet, despite the wishes of some of his more Protestant subjects, he always remained a Catholic. Under Edward VI, the nation was pushed in a strongly Protestant direction; but when he died after only six years on the throne his half-sister Mary, who attempted to re-establish Catholicism, succeeded him. Although her policies struck a chord with some people, many others remained wedded to Protestantism and Mary's policy of open persecution (about 300 Protestants were burnt at the stake between 1555 and 1558) proved counter-productive. The result was that by the time of Mary's death the nation was thoroughly divided; relatively small minorities were deeply attached to either Catholicism or Protestantism, and in between a large middle ground contained many who were ignorant, confused or simply willing to follow the prevailing climate. This was the turbulent situation that the Elizabethan Settlement was intended to regulate and stabilise.

The complex religious history of mid-Tudor England stemmed from the contemporary assumption that the country's official religion would be that of the reigning monarch. On the continent, this principle had been affirmed by the Peace of Augsburg (1555), which established the axiom that a state's religion should be that of its ruler (*cuius regio eius religio*). Elizabeth's fellow Protestants therefore welcomed her accession, acclaiming her as a Protestant heroine. But although Elizabeth's accession ensured that England's official religion would henceforth be Protestant, she had to be sensitive to Catholic feelings and the religious settlement at the beginning of her reign was carefully designed to appeal to as wide a range of opinion as possible. Opposition from Catholic bishops and peers in the House of Lords pushed the queen towards a more conservative settlement. In particular, Elizabeth was named supreme governor of the church; Henry VIII's title of supreme head was not adopted lest Catholics regard it as a usurpation of the pope's title. The new Prayer Book, adopted in 1559, likewise included a form of words in the holy communion that could be read in different ways by both Protestants and Catholics. The church also retained significant echoes of the old church, including bishops, the wearing of clerical vestments, a liturgy in the form of the Prayer Book, and certain elements of ritual in worship – including the sign of the cross in baptism. The settlement thus established a church that, in Conrad Russell's words, 'looked Catholic but sounded Protestant'.[15]

The Elizabethan church settlement was founded on two statutes passed in 1559: the Act of Supremacy and the Act of Uniformity. This provided yet another demonstration of the omnicompetence of statute and the sovereignty of 'Queen-in-Parliament'. The Act of Uniformity enforced the 1559 Prayer Book and enacted penalties for non-attendance at church services. The Act of Supremacy declared that Elizabeth was 'supreme governor . . . as well in all spiritual and ecclesiastical things or causes as temporal'.[16] Although the act ostensibly restored ancient powers to the crown that Mary had renounced, in practice the royal supremacy over the church clearly rested on the authority of statute. One major consequence of this was that parliament henceforth felt able to discuss church matters and offer the queen advice about them, sometimes to a greater extent than Elizabeth was willing to accept.

Whereas Henry VIII's role as supreme head had conferred spiritual powers over the doctrine of the church, as supreme governor Elizabeth's role was more purely secular and administrative; she acted in effect as a lay steward of the church. That nevertheless gave her considerable powers, and despite the parliamentary basis of the supremacy Elizabeth stoutly maintained that these powers were vested in her personally. In particular, she controlled appointments to senior church offices such as bishoprics, and this in turn allowed her to influence the leadership and overall direction of the church. The settlement was rounded off by the promulgation of the Thirty-Nine Articles by Convocation[17] in 1563 (later confirmed by a statute in 1571). Thereafter the queen was determined to prevent any further modification, especially those demanded by the radical Protestants who advocated 'further reformation' to cleanse the church of the lingering echoes of 'popery'. By lending her personal protection to the church, Elizabeth enabled the tender young plant to get established and send down deep roots. As a result, by the end of her reign many could not remember any other pattern of worship and had grown deeply attached to the church and its Prayer Book.

If Elizabeth proved a great friend to the newly established church, the latter was also a powerful support to the crown. Every Sunday a homily on obedience was read from every pulpit, emphasising the duty of obedience to the 'powers that be' and the wickedness of resistance to authority. Monarchy was presented as part of the natural order and an integral link in the 'great chain of being' that descended from God through the whole natural world. The church was in that sense a branch of the state, and one that purveyed highly effective propaganda on the crown's behalf.

The royal supremacy thus gave the monarch considerable influence over the church. Much depended on the ways in which that influence was used. The stability of the church rested to a considerable extent on the monarch's capacity to preserve a balance between those who accepted the church as it was and those who wished to see it reformed, in either a more Catholic or a more

'Puritan' direction. This task required tact, sensitivity and flexibility, for the monarch could not simply expect the entire nation to conform automatically to their own beliefs and practices. In general, Elizabeth and James I managed this very successfully, and it was only after 1625 that Charles I's policies upset the delicate equilibrium which had been carefully fostered within the church.

Conclusions

Throughout this chapter, it has become clear that England in 1558 was very much a personal monarchy. The sovereign was the head of both church and state, and their personality made an immense difference to the conduct of policy and the nature of political life. In many ways, the key to political stability lay in the relationship between the monarch and the leading subjects, above all the nobility and gentry in whose hands lay so much of the responsibility for both national and local government. This was an intensely personal system. In the absence of a written constitution, the boundaries of royal powers – and their relationship with parliament and the rule of law – were necessarily vague and poorly defined, and much depended on mutual trust between the monarch and the political elite. If that trust became eroded, the system lacked any formal means for restoring it. The monarchs wielded considerable powers, but it was not always wise for them to push these to the logical limit; it was possible for monarchs to do things that were legally valid but politically unwise, as Charles I was to discover. The most perceptive rulers – who included Henry VIII and Elizabeth I – recognised that the monarch-in-parliament was more powerful than the monarch alone, and that the secret of successful rule lay in creative collaboration with the political elite. This was the essence of a *dominium politicum et regale*. It was a coherent and organic system, the interlocking nature of which was well summed up in the contemporary metaphor of the 'body politic'. With the right personalities it was perfectly workable, but so personal a system was bound to be heavily dependent on whom the hereditary principle happened to produce as the next monarch. At this date, the English polity had no real constitutional safeguards against the idiosyncrasies of individual rulers, and the accession of a new monarch was always a particularly stressful moment for the 'body politic'. The next chapter will therefore begin by looking more closely at the personality and political style of the woman who assumed the throne in November 1558.

The powers of the monarch in Elizabethan England

1.1 England as a mixed monarchy

From John Aylmer's An harborowe for faithful and true subjects against the late blown blast concerning the government of women*, 1559*

The regiment of England is not a mere monarchy, as some for lack of consideration think, nor a mere oligarchy, nor democracy, but a rule mixed of all these . . . the image whereof, and not the image but the thing indeed, is to be seen in the Parliament House, wherein you shall find these three estates: the King or Queen, which representeth the monarch; the noblemen which be the aristocracy; and the burgesses and knights the democracy . . . If the Parliament use their privileges, the King can ordain nothing without them. If he do, it is his fault in usurping it and their folly in permitting it.

Source: G. R. Elton (ed.), *The Tudor Constitution: documents and commentary*, 2nd edition, Cambridge, 1982, p. 16.

1.2 The prerogatives of the monarch

From Sir Thomas Smith's De republica Anglorum*, 1565*

The monarch of England, king or queen, hath absolutely in his power the authority of war and peace, to defy what prince it shall please him and to bid him to war, and again to reconcile himself and enter into league or truce with him, at his pleasure or the advice only of his privy council. His privy council be chosen also at the prince's pleasure . . . In war time and in the field the prince hath also absolute power, so that his word is law . . . The money is always stamped with the prince's image and title . . . The prince giveth all the chief and highest offices or magistracies of the realm, be it in judgement or dignity, temporal or spiritual . . . All writs, executions and commandments be done in the prince's name . . . The supreme justice is done in the king's name and by his authority only . . . Diverse other rights and preeminences the prince hath which be called prerogatives royal . . . which be declared particularly in the books of the common laws of England.

Source: Elton (ed.), *Tudor Constitution*, pp. 19–20.

1.3 The monarch under the law

From Richard Hooker's Laws of ecclesiastical polity*, c. 1590*

Though no manner [of] person or cause can be unsubject to the king's power, yet so is the power of the king over all and in all limited that unto all his proceedings the law itself is a rule. The axioms of our regal government are these: '*Lex facit regem*' [= the law makes the king]: the king's grant of any favour made contrary to the law is void: '*Rex nihil potest nisi quod iure potest*' [= the king can do nothing but what he can do within the law].

Source: Elton (ed.), *Tudor Constitution*, p. 17.

1.4 The nature and role of parliament

From Richard Hooker's Laws of ecclesiastical polity, *c. 1595*

The Parliament of England . . . is that whereupon the very essence of all government within this kingdom doth depend; it is even the body of the whole realm; it consisteth of the king and of all that within the land are subject unto him; for they are all there present, either in person or by such as they voluntarily have derived their very personal right unto.

Source: Elton (ed.), *Tudor Constitution*, p. 241.

1.5 The subjects' duty of obedience to the monarch

From A homily on obedience, *1547*

Let us mark well and remember that the high power and authority of kings, with their making of laws, judgements and officers, are the ordinances not of man but of God . . . We may not resist, nor in any wise hurt, an anointed king which is God's lieutenant, vicegerent and highest minister in that country where he is king . . . Yet . . . we may not obey kings . . . if they would command us to do anything contrary to God's commandments. In such a case we ought to say with the Apostles: we must rather obey God than man . . . But we must in such cases patiently suffer all wrongs or injuries, referring the judgement of our cause only to God.

Source: Elton (ed.), *Tudor Constitution*, p. 15.

Document case-study questions

1 In 1.1, what reasons does John Aylmer give for not regarding mid-Tudor England as 'a mere monarchy'?

2 What reasons does Sir Thomas Smith give in 1.2 for seeing the monarch's powers as 'absolute'?

3 How far do the ideas expressed by Richard Hooker in 1.3 constitute limitations on royal powers?

4 To what extent are the views of monarchy presented in 1.1–1.3 compatible with each other? In what ways are they contradictory?

5 What light does 1.4 throw on the relationship between the monarch and parliament?

6 What limits on royal actions are implied in 1.5?

Notes and references

1 David Loades, *Power in Tudor England*, London, 1997, p. 9.

2 For some recent analyses of the workings of the court, see, for example, Penry Williams, *The Later Tudors: England, 1547–1603*, Oxford, 1995, pp. 124–31; Christopher Haigh, *Elizabeth I*, Harlow, 1988, pp. 86–105; and David Loades, *Power in Tudor England*, pp. 101–18.

3 G. R. Elton (ed.), *The Tudor Constitution: documents and commentary*, 2nd edition, Cambridge, 1982, p. 14.

4 The best introductions to parliamentary history during Elizabeth's reign are Elton (ed.), *Tudor Constitution*, Chapter 8; Michael A. R. Graves, *Elizabethan parliaments, 1559–1601*, 2nd edition, Harlow, 1996; and T. E. Hartley, *Elizabeth's parliaments: queen, Lords and Commons, 1559–1601*, Manchester, 1992.

5 The royal veto is discussed more fully in Chapter 2, p. 22.

6 Graves, *Elizabethan parliaments*, pp. 64–65, 69–72; Hartley, *Elizabeth's parliaments*, pp. 112–13.

7 These calculations are derived from the dates of Elizabethan parliamentary sessions, printed in Graves, *Elizabethan parliaments*, p. 125.

8 Conrad Russell, *Parliaments and English politics, 1621–1629*, Oxford, 1979, p. 3.

9 Haigh, *Elizabeth I*, pp. 66–67.

10 For useful discussions of the privy council, see especially Elton (ed.), *Tudor Constitution*, pp. 88–116; Haigh, *Elizabeth I*, pp. 66–85; Loades, *Power in Tudor England*, pp. 45–69; and Williams, *Later Tudors*, pp. 131–35.

11 Haigh, *Elizabeth I*, p. 69.

12 Haigh, *Elizabeth I*, pp. 69–70.

13 Haigh, *Elizabeth I*, p. 70.

14 G. R. Elton, *Studies in Tudor and Stuart politics and government*, 4 vols., Cambridge, 1974–92, vol. 4, p. 4.

15 Conrad Russell, 'The Reformation and the creation of the Church of England, 1500–1640', in John Morrill (ed.), *The Oxford illustrated history of Tudor and Stuart Britain*, Oxford, 1996, p. 280.

16 Elton (ed.), *Tudor Constitution*, pp. 344–45; for the Act of Supremacy see pp. 372–77.

17 Convocation was an assembly of clergy that met at the same time as parliament. Within the Church of England, there was a convocation for each of the two provinces, Canterbury and York. The former was the more important, and was often referred to simply as 'Convocation'.

2 Elizabeth I, 1558–1603

Elizabeth's personality

Elizabeth was 25 years old when she succeeded to the throne on 17 November 1558. Her natural intelligence had been evident from an early age. She had been brought up a Protestant and her education was entrusted to several eminent scholars, of whom Roger Ascham was probably the most important. Ascham later wrote that 'her mind has no womanly weakness, her perseverance is equal to that of a man, and her memory long keeps what it quickly picks up'.[1] She had an excellent knowledge of Latin, Greek, French and Italian, and was also talented musically. Although she had received little if any formal political education, her experiences during her half-sister Mary's reign, for much of which she was in effect under house arrest, had taught her about the less attractive side of human nature and schooled her in the arts of pragmatism and survival.

These gifts were allied to a powerful, wilful and determined nature that marked her very clearly as Henry VIII's daughter. The Spanish ambassador, the count of Feria, commented after an interview with Elizabeth early in her reign that 'she seems to me incomparably more feared than her sister and gives her orders and has her way as absolutely as her father did'.[2] Elizabeth was delighted when, during her coronation procession, someone in the crowd cried out 'Remember old King Henry VIII!', and she ensured that the official account emphasised this incident.[3] The queen's imperious streak went along with a flexible and pragmatic approach; throughout her reign Elizabeth tried to keep her options as open as possible, not so much because of indecisiveness as because of a fear that decisive actions would commit her and constrain her freedom of manoeuvre.

One of her most striking qualities was the ability to choose effective counsellors. Her pre-eminent adviser from 1558 until his death in 1598 was William Cecil, Lord Burghley from 1571. Elizabeth appointed him as secretary of state and a privy councillor only three days after her accession, telling him that:

> This judgement I have of you that you will not be corrupted by any manner of gift and that you will be faithful to the state, and that without respect of my private will you will give me that counsel which you think best, and if you shall know anything necessary to be declared to me of secrecy you shall show it to myself only.[4]

Burghley amply lived up to the queen's confidence, and his faithful service was repaid by her loyalty to him. He was not alone in this respect; the first 30 years or so of Elizabeth's reign saw a remarkable continuity of personnel within her close-knit circle of advisers led, in addition to Burghley, by figures such as Robert Dudley, earl of Leicester; Sir Francis Walsingham; Sir Walter Mildmay; and Sir Christopher Hatton. Such length of service helped to generate considerable stability at the heart of government, and the deaths of many of these figures in quick succession in the years around 1590 contributed to the much less settled climate of Elizabeth's later years.

In her handling of parliament and the privy council, Elizabeth displayed a certain manipulative quality. She had many different moods, and could be dictatorial, assertive and emollient by turns. The gender stereotypes of the period attributed such quixotic swings to Elizabeth's womanhood, and some feared the implications of her gender, especially in the earlier part of her reign. Shortly before Elizabeth's accession, John Knox had published his *First blast of the trumpet against the monstrous regiment of women*, and although his views were expressed with extreme bitterness they were widely shared by contemporaries. Even Lord Burghley once remarked that 'there is nothing more fulsome [= offensive] than a she-fool', and in 1560 he commented that diplomatic relations were 'too much for a woman's knowledge'.[5] In 1592 the lord deputy of Ireland complained that 'this fiddling woman troubles me out of measure', and lamented 'God's wounds, this it is to serve a base, bastard, pissing kitchen woman!'[6] As Christopher Haigh has written, 'Elizabeth I was dogged by the fact that she was "only" a woman.'[7] Yet the very fact that Elizabeth achieved all that she did while being a woman enabled her advisers to argue that God smiled on her. At the opening of parliament in 1593, Lord Keeper Puckering said that God 'enableth the weakest sex, and makes them to admire it, that ere now were wont to doubt their good success'.[8] During the course of her reign, there developed a remarkable personality cult that revered the queen as a unique and divinely favoured being.

Elizabeth displayed a striking capacity to transcend her own gender and turn it to advantage. One central way in which she did this was to claim to possess the attributes of a king as well as those of a queen. She declared in 1581 that 'I have the heart of a man, not of a woman, and I am not afraid of anything.'[9] During the Spanish Armada crisis in 1588, she informed the troops assembled at Tilbury that: 'I know I have the body of a weak and feeble woman, but I have the heart and stomach of a king, and of a king of England too.'[10] Elizabeth even turned her failure to marry to advantage by claiming that she had married her subjects; in 1599 she referred to 'all my husbands, my good people'.[11] In *The faerie queene*, Edmund Spenser portrayed Elizabeth as 'Gloriana', 'a most royal queen and empress', while a ballad of 1587[12] described her as:

A monarch maiden Queen
Whose like on earth was never seen.

Elizabeth thus made the very most of the personal aspects of monarchy, presenting herself as a singular creature, part king, part queen, married to her people and blessed by God. It is against the background of this personality cult and public image that Elizabeth's handling of politics needs to be examined.

Parliaments and politics, 1558–85

We saw in the first chapter that in sixteenth-century England political stability depended to a large extent on the relationship between the monarch and the leading subjects, especially those who were members of the privy council and the Great Council of parliament. These people were nearly always deeply loyal to the crown, and committed to preserving England as an independent, Protestant nation-state. Within that framework, however, there was considerable scope for disagreement over how those objectives could be best achieved. When members of the council or parliament stood up to the queen, it was not because they wished to usurp her authority; as Michael Graves has argued, 'there was at no time a struggle for power in the state'.[13] Rather, it was because they wished her to use her powers in certain ways, and because they feared that she was acting against what they saw as the nation's best interests. In particular, they wished to convince Elizabeth that she had a responsibility to marry, to secure the succession, and to protect England from the Catholic menace both at home and abroad.

Elizabeth was not one to be bullied; as she told a parliamentary delegation in November 1566: 'I am your anointed Queen. I will never be by violence constrained to do any thing.'[14] She took the view that members of parliament might freely discuss 'matters of commonwealth' (general social and economic issues), but could only debate 'matters of state' when she invited them to do so. She classified as 'matters of state' anything that touched on her person (such as her marriage or the succession) or on her prerogative as supreme governor in things spiritual or temporal (including the settlement of religion, foreign policy and the granting of monopolies). These were, of course, precisely the subjects that many members most wished to discuss, and the result was a series of disputes over the extent of the Commons' privilege of free speech. Although Elizabeth could curtail debates, she could not prevent them being initiated, and she developed considerable skill in knowing when to hold firm and when to make a tactical retreat.

Marriage and the succession

These issues surfaced earliest in the parliaments of 1563 and 1566–67 in relation to the queen's marriage and the succession. The fact that Elizabeth had nearly succumbed to smallpox in October 1562 generated widespread fears about what might happen if she died without an heir, especially because the nearest claimant to the throne was the Catholic Mary Queen of Scots. The following year, both houses of parliament submitted petitions to Elizabeth arguing that it was her duty to God to marry and settle the succession. Elizabeth responded with an enigmatic speech in which she implied that she did not intend to remain unmarried, but felt that the problem of the succession was too serious to be

settled quickly.[15] Shortly afterwards, she prorogued parliament. Her prevarica-
tion left the issues entirely unresolved, and disquiet continued to rumble on
within the court and council over the years that followed.

It was therefore no surprise that these concerns emerged again when the
parliament reassembled in 1566. The queen reiterated her intention to marry, but
insisted that 'there should not be further talk of that matter'.[16] This prompted one
member, Paul Wentworth, to query whether Elizabeth's response violated the
Commons' privilege of free speech. Some members even wanted to incorporate
the queen's promise to marry and settle the succession into the preamble of the
bill granting financial supply. But in the end, faced with concerted pressure in
both houses, Elizabeth relented; she withdrew her ban on discussion of her
marriage and the succession, remitted one third of the supply that had been
voted, and made a conciliatory closing speech.[17]

This royal emollience might have defused the situation had the Catholic threat
not become dramatically more evident during the years 1568–72. This period
saw the abdication of Mary Queen of Scots and her flight to England (1568);
followed by a rising of the Catholic northern earls on her behalf (1569), a papal
bull excommunicating Elizabeth and absolving her Catholic subjects of their duty
of allegiance (1570), and the Ridolfi Plot in which the duke of Norfolk promised
another rebellion in collaboration with Spain (1571).[18] All these events intensified
Protestant anxieties; and in the parliamentary sessions of 1571 and 1572, privy
councillors orchestrated a co-ordinated campaign calling for Norfolk's
execution, and for Mary to be either attainted or at least excluded from the line
of succession. In the end, Elizabeth reluctantly conceded that Norfolk should die,
but she stood firm over Mary's fate. Although she announced that she could not
accept Mary's attainder, she allowed the houses to proceed with an exclusion
bill. However, she retained the ultimate weapon of the royal veto, and when
this bill was presented to her she refused to give her assent. This was the
'answer answerless' that Elizabeth always held up her sleeve.

It is important to remember, however, that Elizabeth's use of the veto on major
political or constitutional questions was relatively rare. During the whole of her
reign, although she vetoed about 70 of the 506 bills presented to her, fewer than
10 of these were vetoed because they invaded the royal prerogative or conflicted
with her preferred policies. In the overwhelming majority of cases, the queen
vetoed bills promoted by private individuals or groups that conflicted with other
interests. The fact that she vetoed legislation is therefore not in itself a useful
index of political friction between crown and parliament, or a sign that she was
having to thwart parliamentary attempts to limit her authority.[19]

Friction was nevertheless very real at times, and when the houses returned to
the issues of marriage and the succession in 1576 they prompted another major
confrontation over the right of free speech. Again, the queen let it be known that
she did not want the Commons to discuss these matters, and this time Peter
Wentworth – brother of Paul – launched a bitter attack on the way in which
'rumours and messages' were used to inhibit debate. This came so close to
personal criticism of Elizabeth that the house stopped Wentworth and

imprisoned him in the Tower.[20] Although he may have expressed in an extreme form what some other members inwardly felt but did not dare say, few wished to be associated with Wentworth's outburst, and the evidence suggests that he was essentially working alone. Indeed, when he raised similar questions in 1587, the Commons was so reluctant to support him that the queen and the privy council were able to imprison him during the session without causing widespread protest within the house (unlike the case of William Strickland, p. 26, below).

Mary Queen of Scots

Probably more prevalent than the Wentworth brothers' obsession with freedom of speech, certainly among privy councillors, were continuing fears for Elizabeth's personal safety and a desire to neutralise the threat from Mary Queen of Scots. The assassination of William of Orange in July 1584 concentrated minds on just how much England's preservation as an independent Protestant state depended upon Elizabeth's survival. The following autumn, Burghley and Walsingham led the council in promoting the Bond of Association, a voluntary oath that bound its signatories to pursue and kill anyone who tried to harm the queen, and also to execute any 'pretended successor' on behalf of whom such an attempt was made.[21] The heirs of such pretenders were to be excluded from the line of succession. Significantly, provision was also made for the continued operation of government in the event of the queen's death. The powers of the crown were to be assumed by the privy council – strengthened by senior officers of state, senior judges and certain members of the House of Lords – to form a Great Council of 30 persons. Parliament was to be summoned to meet within 20 days, take over supreme authority and choose a successor. In effect, the monarchy was to continue to run on auto-pilot. During such an interregnum, England would be a monarchy without a monarch – what Patrick Collinson has called 'a monarchical republic'.[22]

Elizabeth, however, strongly disapproved of some of these terms, and when parliament met in November 1584 she successfully blocked Burghley's attempts to translate them into statute. The 'Act for the surety of the Queen's person' did not make any provision for the continued legal operation of government during an interregnum, mainly because Elizabeth felt that this would compromise royal authority. She also ensured that James VI of Scotland was specifically exempted from the penalties imposed on the heirs of any 'pretended successor'. The act thus modified the terms of the Bond of Association and, as Michael Graves has written, 'as so often happened, the complete fulfilment of [the queen's councillors'] objectives was frustrated chiefly by their royal mistress'.[23]

The perceived threat from Mary Queen of Scots nevertheless remained. Towards the end of 1583, the Throckmorton Plot to assassinate Elizabeth and place Mary on the throne was uncovered. In the summer of 1586 Mary was implicated in the Babington Plot, a conspiracy to kill Elizabeth in which Mary was in effect 'framed' by Walsingham. The following autumn a special commission found her guilty of high treason. At the end of October, pressure from Burghley and the other privy councillors led Elizabeth reluctantly to recall parliament, and almost immediately a co-ordinated bicameral campaign (that is, one involving members of both houses) was launched calling for Mary's execution. It was another classic example of conciliar pressure on the queen being extended to the wider forum of parliament. For weeks Elizabeth prevaricated, and even when she finally signed the death warrant on 1 February 1587 she did not authorise it to be implemented. At this point, Burghley took the initiative and with the collusion of other councillors ordered the secretary to the council, William Davison, to put the warrant into effect. Mary was executed at Fotheringhay Castle on 8 February.

Elizabeth was furious when she learned of this. A combination of respect for another monarch and fear of foreign reprisals had inclined her to the very last to hold out against Mary's execution. Burghley's behaviour led to the most serious row between him and Elizabeth during the entire reign. For four months he stayed away from court while Davison was made a scapegoat and imprisoned in the Tower. Elizabeth's councillors had overridden her personal preferences, but they had acted from deeply loyal motives. They wished to remove a perceived threat to Elizabeth's life, on which English Protestantism and national independence were thought to hang. Once again, apparent 'opposition' to the queen was motivated by a wish to protect her – and the nation's – interests from her own inclinations and inaction, rather than by any desire to usurp or limit her authority.

Elizabeth's reluctance to see Mary executed stemmed in part from a fear of antagonising the Catholic powers on the continent, especially Spain. This brings us to Elizabeth's foreign policy, which was the aspect of government in which she enjoyed the greatest measure of autonomy from her council and parliament.

Foreign policy

In this period, international relations were seen very much in terms of the personal and dynastic interactions between individual rulers rather than of relationships between states. The power to make war or peace was an accepted part of the royal prerogative, and this was another area which Elizabeth included among 'matters of state' that she did not wish parliament to discuss unless she invited them to do so.

Elizabeth inherited a difficult international situation. Shortly after her accession, the two great Catholic powers in Western Europe, France and Spain, made peace at Cateau-Cambrésis (April 1559). This meant that England's likeliest potential enemies on the continent were free to wage war against her, and Elizabeth wisely decided that her primary aim should be to avoid antagonising her near neighbours. Some of her advisers, led by Leicester and Walsingham, strongly urged the queen to lend support to the Protestant (Huguenot) minority in France, and to support the Dutch Protestants who rebelled against Spanish rule from 1566 onwards. However, Elizabeth – with Burghley's support – resolved to avoid foreign entanglements for as long as possible. She was prepared to turn a blind eye to the depredations of English pirates, such as Francis Drake, on Spanish ships using routes to and from the

New World. But only in 1585, by the Treaty of Nonsuch, did she finally commit England to assisting the Dutch directly. She agreed to send 6,400 infantry, 1,000 cavalry and £126,000 a year until the war ended.[24] In the event, the war dragged on until the year after Elizabeth's death. It cast a shadow over the last 18 years of her reign and took a toll on England's government, economy and society that marked a new and distinct phase in the reign (see pp. 28–32).

Elizabeth's hesitation caused frustration among some of her critics, for example Sir Walter Raleigh, who complained that she 'did all by halves'.[25] But with hindsight, she was probably wise to avoid the strains of war for as long as possible. More generally, the disputes between her and her advisers, in council and parliament, should be seen as a series of running debates over how best to serve England's interests rather than as part of any attempt to limit the crown's powers. There was no organised 'opposition', and no fundamental constitutional changes were proposed or adopted during the reign. Through all the discussion of particular issues and policies, the basic structural relationship between crown and parliament was not significantly altered.

Religion and the church, 1558–85

A similar lack of institutional change was also evident in the Church of England during these years. However, this was certainly not for lack of trying by some of Elizabeth's subjects and it reflected the queen's determination to maintain the Elizabethan Settlement essentially unchanged. She closely guarded her status as supreme governor of the church and saw any attempt to change the church as a personal attack on her. She even regarded discussion of the nature of the church as an encroachment on the royal prerogative. In defending this position she faced two main threats: one came from those 'hotter sort of Protestants' often called 'Puritans' by their critics, and the other came from the Catholic community. This section will analyse each problem, and Elizabeth's response to it, in turn.

The Puritans

Although there was never an organised 'puritan movement', the term 'Puritan' remains a helpful label for those godly Protestants who regarded the Elizabethan church as 'but halfly reformed', and wished to cleanse it of all echoes of the pre-Reformation church. These echoes included bishops, the wearing of vestments, the Prayer Book and the retention of certain rituals such as the sign of the cross in baptism. Almost from the beginning of her reign, Elizabeth faced pressure from such people to complete what they saw as an unfinished reformation; and always she deflected them, insisting the church settlement should not be modified.

The earliest attempts at 'puritan' reform came in the parliamentary sessions of 1566–67 and 1571 in the form of the 'alphabetical bills' (so called because they were labelled A–F in the *Commons' journal*). These were in particular designed to improve the quality of the clergy by attacking pluralism, absenteeism and corrupt practices. There is evidence that certain members of the Council, and possibly even some bishops, lent them support.[26] However, the queen made her disapproval very plain, and the Lords quickly backed off in the face of this. In the Commons in 1571, William Strickland promoted a bill allowing Protestant ministers to deviate from the Prayer Book by dropping certain allegedly 'popish' vestiges from the past. On the queen's instructions, the privy council ordered him to be detained. There was an immediate outcry in the Commons at what appeared to be a breach of members' privilege of freedom from arrest while parliament was sitting. The queen climbed down, allowed him to return to the house, and thereafter carefully avoided doing anything that might seem to breach this privilege without the Commons' consent. But although she backed off over Strickland, she successfully blocked the proposed bills, and only that enacting the Thirty-Nine Articles (adopted by Convocation in 1563) actually became a statute in 1571.[27]

The failure of attempted reform by statute led to a more aggressive 'puritan' effort in the parliamentary session of 1572. This took the form of two *Admonitions to parliament*, which presented blueprints for reforming the church along presbyterian lines that would have brought it much closer to the Calvinist churches of Scotland or the continent. The first *Admonition* was written by two London ministers, John Field and Thomas Wilcox; the second by the Lady Margaret professor of divinity at Cambridge, Thomas Cartwright.[28] Once again, Elizabeth dug her heels in, and in May 1572 she banned further parliamentary discussion of religious bills.[29]

Following this rebuff, there were no more attempts to reform the church through parliament for over a decade. Instead, 'puritan' clergy tried to reform the church from within, for example by organising local meetings of clergy ('prophesyings') to discuss biblical texts. The queen regarded these meetings as subversive and thought them likely to become presbyterian cells. She ordered Edmund Grindal, archbishop of Canterbury from 1576, to suppress them, and when he refused she suspended him. On Grindal's death in 1583 she replaced him with the strongly anti-Puritan John Whitgift.

The final really significant instances of 'puritan' pressure through parliament during Elizabeth's reign were the 'bill and book' campaigns of the mid-1580s. In 1584, Peter Turner presented a bill to replace the Prayer Book with the Genevan liturgy, to abolish episcopacy and to establish a presbyterian structure of pastors, lay elders and assemblies. The privy councillors in the Commons set their face firmly against this proposal and it was dropped. Two years later, in the parliament of 1586–87, Anthony Cope introduced a revised version of the proposal, urging the adoption of a book of discipline that laid down a detailed scheme of church government based on elders and pastors at parochial level, classes at regional level and synods at national level. The Genevan Prayer Book was to be adopted. Once again, the privy councillors attempted to scotch the scheme, warning that it would incur the queen's wrath, but the Commons overruled them. The queen intervened, and ordered five of the radical leaders (including Peter Wentworth) to be sent to the Tower, where they remained for the rest of the session. With them gone, the privy councillors were able to ensure the defeat of Cope's 'bill and book'.[30]

Elizabeth's concept of her royal supremacy, and her strong desire to prevent parliamentary discussion of church reform, were well summed up in a draft message prepared for parliament in 1587. One section was headed 'Why you ought not to deal in matters of religion', and included the passage: 'Her Majesty taketh your petition to be against the prerogative of the Crown. For by your full consents it hath been confirmed and enacted . . . that the full power, jurisdiction and supremacy in Church causes . . . should be united and annexed to the imperial crown of this realm.'[31] This remained her sense of the monarchy's powers in matters spiritual throughout her reign, and she succeeded in defending them very effectively.

The Catholics

The 'puritan' challenge largely receded after 1587, and by this time attention was primarily focused on the Catholic threat. This presented the queen and the political elite with a rather different set of problems. At the time of Elizabeth's accession, the majority of the English Catholic community accepted her as their sovereign. They were happy to distinguish between their spiritual allegiance to the pope and their temporal allegiance to Elizabeth and preferred not to make trouble for the new regime. This suited Elizabeth very well. The 1559 Act of Uniformity levied a fine of 12 pence a week on 'recusants' (those who failed to attend the services of the established church), but enforcement of this was very patchy during the 1560s. Francis Bacon famously praised Elizabeth for 'not liking to make windows into men's hearts and secret thoughts', and a proclamation of 1570 promised no investigation of those whose conduct was 'not manifestly repugnant and obstinate to the laws of the realm'.[32] In principle, Elizabeth was willing to leave Catholics in peace provided that they did not present a political threat to her.

Unfortunately, the events of 1568–71 (Mary's arrival, the Northern Rising, the papal bull and the Ridolfi Plot) drastically changed this situation and made many of Elizabeth's advisers regard Catholics, both at home and abroad, as natural enemies. This also coincided with the arrival in England, from the later 1560s, of Catholic missionary priests trained on the continent. The result was that the remainder of the reign saw a series of increasingly draconian penal laws against Catholics. These were motivated by self-defence and a necessary protection of national security, but the influence of some of Elizabeth's more strongly Protestant advisers – such as Walsingham, Leicester and also to a lesser extent Burghley – gave them a vindictive edge born of anti-Catholic zeal.

The gradual escalation of this punitive legislation was relentless, and illustrated the unrestrained powers of statute to define and redefine the law of treason. In 1571, in response to Elizabeth's excommunication, it was made treasonable to bring in or publish any documents from Rome. A further act of 1581 extended the treason law to cover all those who sought to withdraw subjects from their allegiance to either the queen or the Church of England, and raised the recusancy fine to £20. In 1585 it was made treason even to be the cause for which others plotted treason; while another act ordered the driving out of all Jesuits and seminary priests from England, and made it treason to be convicted of being either. Finally, in 1593 an act compelled known Catholics to remain within five miles of their home and to register themselves there.[33]

All of this penal legislation was pressed by some of the queen's advisers and their allies in the Commons. Elizabeth herself remained unenthusiastic about it and found herself pushed reluctantly into accepting it. She was less paranoid about the Catholic menace than many members of her council and parliament, and seems to have genuinely disliked the idea of persecution. She also seems to have realised (possibly remembering her half-sister's experience) that persecution was likely to be counter-productive and that few things strengthen any cause so effectively as the creation of martyrs. She was responsible for the reduction of penalties against recusants in the 1581 act; and the following year Leicester complained that 'nothing in this world grieveth me more than to see her Majesty believes this increase of papists in her realm can be no danger to her'.[34] To godly Protestants, this was another cause for concern about Elizabeth and how effectively she was defending England's interests. The queen was able to slow down the pressure for anti-Catholic persecution, but she could not avoid it entirely; nor is it likely that she wished to go to that extreme. Furthermore, from 1585 the situation changed once again as England found itself committed to military intervention on the continent against Spain. Henceforth England was at war and Catholics at home could be regarded as potential 'fifth-columnists'. This was one aspect of a complex series of changes which has led some historians to see the years around 1585 as a watershed that brought the Elizabethan heyday to an end and ushered in the queen's 'second reign'.[35]

Elizabeth's 'second reign', 1585–1603

The changing context

A combination of circumstances makes it appropriate to speak of a 'second reign'. Warfare after 1585 imposed considerable stress on a pre-modern economy that lacked the tax structure to mobilise resources efficiently. These demands, aggravated by dearth and disease, led to widespread hardship and shortages. This, together with the crown's increased demands for parliamentary supply, caused growing political strain. The system was further weakened by the deaths of many of Elizabeth's most reliable advisers in the late 1580s and early 1590s; and by the emergence of two younger, thrusting figures, Robert Cecil and the earl of Essex, whose rivalry promoted factional conflict of a kind not seen hitherto. Over all these difficulties presided the ageing figure of Elizabeth; although her mental faculties remained unimpaired, her grip on affairs began to loosen and she showed signs of growing out of touch with her subjects. This was brutally brought home to her by the turbulent parliaments of 1597–98 and 1601, and by Essex's attempted coup of 1601. Her constitutional position was not affected, but her exercise of it began to decline. Unchanged in their fundamentals, the powers of the monarchy were managed somewhat less effectively than in the first 30 years of the reign.

This sense of *fin de siècle* decline cannot be blamed on the queen alone. Nearly 20 years of sustained warfare imposed a severe burden on a state whose fiscal system was virtually unchanged since the fourteenth century. In all, between 1585 and 1603, over 100,000 men were conscripted for military service overseas, and the wars cost around £4,500,000 at a time when the ordinary revenues of the crown were no more than £300,000 a year.[36] The result was a dramatic increase in the crown's requests for parliamentary supply. Whereas only nine subsidies were voted in the three decades from 1559 to 1589, no fewer than ten were voted between 1593 and 1601 (three in 1593, three in 1597, and four in 1601). The crown also collected benevolences from office-holders in 1594 and 1599, and also forced loans in 1588, 1590 and 1597.[37] These were special levies of money – raised by prerogative authority in a national emergency, such as wartime – and subsequently confirmed by parliament. It is interesting to note that at this date, and in such an evident emergency, there was no challenge to the crown's constitutional right to raise these taxes, in marked contrast to what was to happen under Charles I in the 1620s (see p. 60).

Unfortunately, the country was ill equipped to respond to such heavy financial demands. During the later sixteenth and early seventeenth centuries the value of the parliamentary subsidy steadily declined, from £120,000 in 1585 to £85,000 by 1601, and to only £55,000 by 1628. The main reason for this decrease was chronic under-assessment of the political elite. Members of the nobility and gentry were responsible, as subsidy commissioners, for assessing each other; many used this as a form of patronage and gave low assessments to their friends. There was also no thorough way of updating the lists of those who paid the subsidy, with the result that taxpayers were not replaced as they died. England's capacity to pay taxes was further eroded by the serious disruption of trade with the continent during wartime. This produced widespread hardship, especially among those who worked in the cloth industry (cloth was England's principal export). These problems were compounded by the misfortune of a series of bad harvests, in 1585, 1586, 1589, 1590, 1594, 1595, 1596, 1597 and 1601. The four summers of 1594–97 saw the four worst English harvests of the whole sixteenth century. In a primarily agrarian economy this was little short of disastrous. To make matters even worse, there was an outbreak of plague in 1593, and the dislocation of war contributed to the spread of diseases associated with under-nourishment in 1596–98. Such setbacks placed the whole system under severe strain and generated growing political unrest.

The regime was handicapped in its response to these problems by the deaths, in very quick succession, of many of Elizabeth's most experienced advisers, many of whom had been prominent in her counsels since the beginning of the reign. The deaths of Leicester (1588), Mildmay (1589), Walsingham (1590), Warwick (1590) and Hatton (1591) marked the passing of many of the queen's own generation. Although Burghley lived on until 1598, and remained dedicated and industrious to the last, from the early 1590s he was increasingly incapacitated by illness. Elizabeth had always relied on a small, close-knit group of advisers and found it difficult to replace these key figures.

The Cecil–Essex rivalry

Into the vacuum left by these deaths stepped two younger, intensely ambitious figures: Burghley's second son, Robert Cecil; and Robert Devereux, earl of Essex. Although in one sense these two Roberts sought to assume the mantles of Burghley and Leicester, at another level they represented an entirely different political generation and culture. Burghley and Leicester had co-existed in a friendly way, and their political differences of emphasis had been played out in a context of profound loyalty to the regime. Their greatest fear had been the collapse of an independent, Protestant England; they may have differed over how best to avoid that, but both preferred to bury their differences rather than risk destabilising the regime. Neither wished to see a return to the turbulence of the reigns of Edward VI and Mary. By contrast, Robert Cecil and Essex had both been born after Elizabeth's accession (in 1563 and 1566 respectively). Lacking experience of how wrong things had gone before 1558, they were less cautious about rocking the boat. Unlike Elizabeth's own contemporaries, they also realised that their political futures were not entirely bound up with the queen's survival; both could reasonably expect to outlive her by many years and therefore needed to carve out their own political futures.

It was hardly surprising that the queen never felt an intuitive rapport with this new generation of figures who were young enough to be her children. She was ageing and found it difficult to adapt to a changed political world. A German traveller, Paul Hentzner, left a haunting description[38] of Elizabeth's appearance in a court procession in 1598:

> next came the Queen, in the 65th year of her age (as we were told), very majestic, her face oblong, fair but wrinkled; her eyes small, yet black and pleasant; her nose a little hooked, her lips narrow, and her teeth black . . . her hair was of an auburn colour, but false.

Right to the very end, she remained determined to keep up appearances. Artists were not permitted to portray her as she really looked but instead required to depict a youthful appearance based on an official stencil outline of her face that was issued to them. Determined efforts were made to destroy any unflattering images. Yet there was no hiding the brutal truth: as the queen grew older her grip on political affairs slowly started to loosen. She had always tried to keep her options open, but in the later years of her reign her dithering began to leave her somewhat marginalised, especially as the demands of war forced others to take urgent strategic decisions. For the first time, she grew out of touch with the kingdom at large.

This was all the more significant because the rise of Cecil and Essex ushered in a new political culture based upon much more aggressive factional conflict. As Simon Adams has argued, until the 1590s political groupings were so fluid as scarcely to deserve the name 'factions'; but in that decade 'factions became the norm of Court politics rather than the exception. The politics of collegiality were replaced by the politics of competition.'[39] Whereas Burghley and Leicester had dispensed their patronage to many of the same individuals, with no feeling of hostility, Cecil and Essex jealously guarded their hold over their clients and refused to reward the followers of the other. Both of them assembled bodies of supporters, including in parliament, and appointments to public offices (such as lord warden of the Cinque Ports in 1597) provoked bitter tussles between the favoured candidates of each faction.

In this increasingly cut-throat competition Cecil's industry and professionalism ultimately proved far more successful than Essex's somewhat superficial glamour. The feud moved into its most intense phase after Burghley's death in August 1598. Essex became progressively more paranoid and complained of being marginalised, especially during 1599 when he was away in Ireland leading a disastrous expedition against the Catholic rebel forces of the earl of Tyrone. On his return, after abandoning his command without the queen's permission, Essex was placed under house arrest, and in the autumn of 1600 the non-renewal of his lease of customs revenues from imported sweet wines provided further evidence of the collapse of his political position.

For Essex this was the final straw. On 7 February 1601 he paid for a production of Shakespeare's *Richard II* (a play with deeply uncomfortable connotations for the queen and her councillors) and the following day he launched an attempted coup in London, ostensibly directed against the 'Cecilians'. This went catastrophically wrong; outside his inner circle, he failed to win the support he had expected among the nobility and the London populace. His followers proved too scattered to offer him serious help and the revolt collapsed within hours. Essex was convicted of high treason, and was executed on 25 February.

In one sense this fiasco was the product of Essex's own deeply neurotic personality and, by the beginning of 1601, he seems to have been on the verge of a breakdown. But for the queen possibly the most disturbing aspect of the whole episode was the evidence it revealed of discontent within the political elite. Wisely, she did not launch a vendetta against Essex's accomplices, most of whom – including the earls of Southampton, Rutland and Bedford – were spared. But although few wished to follow Essex into open insurrection, many found the incessant financial and human costs of the war increasingly crushing. Concern about the regime's management of the wartime economy added to the unrest, which burst into the open in the troubled parliaments of 1597–98 and 1601.

Elizabeth's final years

The principal targets of hostility in these parliaments were monopolies. These were grants by which the crown gave particular individuals the sole right to manufacture certain commodities (e.g. starch, cloth or bottles) or to market them (e.g. fish, salt or coal). This enabled the monopolists to drive prices upwards, and they were therefore blamed for making wartime hardship even worse. The problem for parliament was that the right to grant monopolies lay within the royal prerogative. In 1597–98, Elizabeth prevaricated as members protested against monopolies. When they submitted a petition complaining of the abuses, she promised that obnoxious monopolies would be tried at law, but that she would always guard her prerogative as 'the chiefest flower in her garland'.[40] But although some grants were repealed or tried in court, in practice little changed.

The result was that when parliament reassembled in October 1601 there was what David Dean has called 'the most significant outburst of opposition in any Elizabethan Parliament'.[41] Member after member bitterly denounced monopolies, echoing Robert Wingfield's complaint that 'the wound . . . is still bleeding'.[42] But members hesitated over whether to proceed by a bill, lest that encroach upon the royal prerogative. Essentially, they were mounting a powerful verbal campaign to persuade the queen to use her powers in ways they wished, rather than trying to limit or abolish those powers. Fortunately, Elizabeth recognised that the time had come to make concessions, and on 30 November she issued a proclamation cancelling the most unpopular monopolies (including those for the making or selling of salt, vinegar, pots, brushes, bottles and starch) and referring grievances concerning the rest to the common law courts.

Two days later Elizabeth addressed the Commons and delivered what came to be known as her 'golden speech'. It was a masterpiece of conciliation, in which she thanked members for their loyalty and 'zeal to their countries', and assured them that 'never thought was cherished in my heart that tended not to my people's good'.[43] Several different versions of this speech survive, and in what was probably the official version Elizabeth affirmed her prerogative right to reward whoever she chose.[44] By taking action against hated monopolies while affirming her right in principle to issue them, she forged a compromise that defused the crisis and preserved her own powers intact.

Although Elizabeth lived on until 24 March 1603, this final speech to her last parliament provides an appropriate point at which to draw this chapter to a close. It reveals that even in her later years the queen retained her shrewdness and mastery of public relations. Her political instincts and her judgement of when to make concessions remained sound. Above all, the parliament of 1601 illustrated yet again the profoundly important role that the monarch's personal skills played in early modern England. Those abilities were vital in shaping the relationship between the crown and the political elite, and without them stability was likely to become eroded – as the reigns of some of Elizabeth's successors were to demonstrate all too clearly.

Document case study
Parliamentary 'opposition' to Elizabeth I

2.1 Elizabeth relents and allows discussion of the succession in 1566

From the Commons' journals collected by Sir Simonds D'Ewes

11 November: Paul Wentworth . . . desired to know whether the Queen's command and inhibition that they should no longer dispute of the matter of succession (sent yesterday to the House) was not against the privileges and liberties of the said House . . .

12 November: Mr Speaker [reported that] he had received a special command from her

Highness to this House, notwithstanding her first commandment [to the same effect], that there should not be further talk of that matter in the House (touching the declaration of a successor in case that her Majesty should die without issue) and if any person thought himself not satisfied but had further reasons, let him come before the Privy Council and there show them . . .

25 November: Mr Speaker . . . declared her Highness' pleasure to be that for her good will to the House she did revoke her two former commandments requiring the House no further to proceed at this time in the matter. Which revocation was taken of all the House most joyfully, with most hearty prayer and thanks for the same.

Source: G. R. Elton (ed.), *The Tudor Constitution: documents and commentary*, 2nd edition, Cambridge, 1982, pp. 317–18.

2.2 William Strickland's bill for reforming the Prayer Book provokes debate in 1571

From the Commons' journals collected by Sir Simonds D'Ewes

20 April: Mr Treasurer [warned the Commons] to be wary in our proceedings, and neither to venture further than our assured warrant might stretch, nor to hazard our good opinion with her Majesty on any doubtful cause . . . He further said that [Strickland] was in no sort stayed [= detained] for any word or speech by him in that place offered, but for the exhibiting of a bill into the House against the prerogative of the Queen, which was not to be tolerated . . .

Mr Yelverton said . . . that all matters not treason, or too much to the derogation of the imperial crown, were tolerable there [in the Commons] where all things came to be considered of . . . That to say the Parliament had no power to determine of the Crown was high treason . . . He showed it was fit for princes to have their prerogatives; but yet the same to be straitened within reasonable limits. The prince, he showed, could not of herself make laws; neither might she by the same reason break laws . . .

Source: Elton (ed.), *Tudor Constitution*, pp. 319–20.

2.3 Peter Wentworth strongly defends the Commons' privilege of free speech, 1576

From the Commons' journals collected by Sir Simonds D'Ewes

Amongst other, Mr Speaker, two things do great hurt in this place . . . the one is a rumour which runneth about the House and this it is, 'Take heed what you do, the Queen's Majesty liketh not such a matter. Whosoever prefereth it, she will be offended with him'. Or the contrary, 'Her Majesty liketh of such matter. Whosoever speaketh against it, she will be much offended with him'.

The other: sometimes a message is brought into the House, either of commanding or inhibiting, very injurious to the freedom of speech and consultation. I would to God, Mr Speaker, that these two were buried in hell, I mean rumours and messages, for wicked undoubtedly they are . . .

Upon this speech the House, out of a reverent regard of her Majesty's honour, stopped his further proceeding before he had fully finished his speech . . . It was ordered . . . that the said Peter Wentworth should be committed close prisoner to the Tower for his said offence.

Source: Michael A. R. Graves, *Elizabethan parliaments, 1559–1601*, 2nd edition, Harlow, 1996, pp. 114–15.

2.4 Anthony Cope prompts debate in the parliament of 1587 by proposing a 'bill and book' that would have overturned the Elizabethan Settlement and introduced a radically revised Prayer Book

From the Commons' journals collected by Sir Simonds D'Ewes

Mr Speaker in effect used this speech: for that her Majesty before this time had commanded the House not to meddle with this matter, and that her Majesty had promised to take order in those causes, he doubted not but to the good satisfaction of all her people, he desired that it would please them to spare the reading of it. Notwithstanding the House desired the reading of it. Whereupon Mr Speaker willed the clerk to read it . . . Mr Dalton made a motion against the reading of it, saying that it was not meet to be read . . . and thought that this dealing would bring her Majesty's indignation against the House thus to enterprise the dealing with those things which her Majesty especially had taken into her own charge and discretion. Whereupon Mr Lewknor spake, . . . and thought it very fit that the petition and book should be read. [Mr Hurleston and Mr Bainbridge supported Mr Lewknor's view.]

On Thursday . . . Mr Cope, Mr Lewknor, Mr Hurleston and Mr Bainbridge were sent for to my Lord Chancellor and by divers of the Privy Council, and from thence were sent to the Tower.

Source: Graves, *Elizabethan parliaments*, pp. 108–9.

2.5 Elizabeth I's views on the Commons' claims to freedom of speech

From the lord keeper's response to the speaker's petition at the beginning of the 1593 parliament

Her Majesty granteth you liberal but not licentious speech, liberty therefore but with due limitation . . . It shall be meet therefore that each man of you contain his speech within the bounds of loyalty and good discretion . . . For liberty of speech her Majesty commandeth me to tell you that to say yea or no to bills, God forbid that any man should be restrained or afraid to answer according to his best liking, with some short declaration of his reason therein, and therein to have a free voice, which is the very true liberty of the House; not, as some suppose, to speak there of all causes as him listeth [= pleases], and to frame a form of religion or a state of government as to their idle brains shall seem meetest [= fittest].

Source: Elton (ed.), *Tudor Constitution*, p. 274.

2.6 Elizabeth bows to parliamentary pressure to introduce measures against monopolies, 1601

From the Commons' journals collected by Sir Simonds D'Ewes

25 November: Mr Speaker . . . spake to this effect: [the queen] yields you all hearty thanks for your care and special regard of those things that concern her state . . . , for our loyalty . . . She said that partly by limitation of her Council, and partly by divers petitions that have been delivered unto her . . . , she understood that divers patents which she had granted were grievous to her subjects . . . But she said that she had never assented to grant anything which was *malum in se* [= evil in itself]; and if in the abuse of her grant there be anything evil . . . she herself would take present order of reformation . . . Further order should be taken presently and not *in futuro* [= in the future] . . . and that some should be presently repealed, some suspended, and none put in execution but such as should first have a trial according to the law for the good of the people . . .

Source: Elton (ed.), *Tudor Constitution*, pp. 324–25.

Document case-study questions

1 To what extent does 2.1 show Elizabeth I making a concession to parliament?

2 What limitations on royal powers are discussed in 2.2?

3 How far does 2.3 contain personal criticism of the queen?

4 In what ways does 2.4 constitute 'opposition' to the crown?

5 Comment on the views expressed in 2.5.

6 What light does 2.6 shed on Elizabeth's handling of parliament?

7 Using these sources and your wider knowledge, consider whether relations between Elizabeth and her parliaments were characterised more by harmony or by conflict.

Notes and references

1 Penry Williams, *The later Tudors: England, 1547–1603*, Oxford, 1995, p. 230.

2 Williams, *Later Tudors*, p. 230.

3 Christopher Haigh, *Elizabeth I*, Harlow, 1988, p. 21.

4 Michael A. R. Graves, *Burghley: William Cecil, Lord Burghley*, Harlow, 1998, p. 30.

5 Graves, *Burghley*, p. 89.

6 Haigh, *Elizabeth I*, p. 9.

7 Haigh, *Elizabeth I*, p. 9.

8 T. E. Hartley (ed.), *Proceedings in the parliaments of Elizabeth I*, 3 vols., Leicester, 1981–95, vol. 3, p. 20.

9 Haigh, *Elizabeth I*, pp. 21–22.

10 Wallace MacCaffrey, *Elizabeth I*, London, 1993, p. 22.

11 Haigh, *Elizabeth I*, p. 20.

12 Haigh, *Elizabeth I*, pp. 20, 86–87.

13 Graves, *Burghley*, p. 93.

14 Hartley (ed.), *Proceedings*, vol. 1, p. 148.

15 Hartley (ed.), *Proceedings*, vol. 1, pp. 94–95.

16 *Commons' journal*, vol. 1, p. 77.

17 See Source 2.1.

18 For a good overview of these events, see Williams, *Later Tudors*, pp. 253–65.

19 G. R. Elton, *The parliament of England, 1559–1581*, Cambridge, 1986, pp. 123–26; T. E. Hartley, *Elizabeth's parliaments: queen, Lords and Commons, 1559–1601*, Manchester, 1992, p. 121.

20 See Source 2.3. For the speech, see Hartley (ed.), *Proceedings*, vol. 1, pp. 425–34; for an analysis of it, see Hartley, *Elizabeth's parliaments*, pp. 127–34.

21 Graves, *Burghley*, p. 74.

22 Patrick Collinson, *Elizabethan essays*, London, 1994, pp. 48–56.

23 Graves, *Burghley*, p. 74.

24 Williams, *Later Tudors*, pp. 534–35.

25 Williams, *Later Tudors*, p. 535.

26 Elton, *Parliament of England*, pp. 205–10.

27 Elton, *Parliament of England*, pp. 207–14.

28 For abridged versions of the texts of the *Admonitions*, see G. R. Elton (ed.), *The Tudor Constitution: documents and commentary*, 2nd edition, Cambridge, 1982, pp. 448–52.

29 Hartley (ed.), *Proceedings*, vol. 1, pp. 373–79.

30 On the 'bill and book' campaigns, see David Dean, *Law-making and society in late Elizabethan England: the parliament of England, 1584–1601*, Cambridge, 1996, pp. 98–103.

31 Hartley, *Elizabeth's parliaments*, p. 95.

32 Haigh, *Elizabeth I*, p. 37.

33 For a discussion of this body of penal legislation, including extensive extracts from the principal statutes, see Elton (ed.), *Tudor Constitution*, pp. 419–42.

34 Haigh, *Elizabeth I*, p. 39.

35 For the idea of Elizabeth's 'second reign', see especially John Guy (ed.), *The reign of Elizabeth I: court and culture in the last decade*, Cambridge, 1995.

36 Christopher Haigh, 'Politics in an age of peace and war, 1570–1630', in John Morrill (ed.), *The Oxford illustrated history of Tudor and Stuart England*, Oxford, 1996, p. 338.

37 Haigh, 'Politics in an age of peace and war', pp. 341–42.

38 Williams, *Later Tudors*, p. 327.

39 Simon Adams, 'The patronage of the crown in Elizabethan politics: the 1590s in perspective', in Guy (ed.), *The reign of Elizabeth I*, p. 45.

40 Williams, *Later Tudors*, p. 363.

41 Dean, *Law-making and society*, p. 91.

42 Hartley, *Elizabeth's parliaments*, p. 148.

43 Elton (ed.), *Tudor Constitution*, p. 326.

44 For the different surviving versions of the 'golden speech', see Hartley (ed.), *Proceedings*, vol. 3, pp. 288–97, 412–14, 494–96. The texts are discussed in Hartley, *Elizabeth's parliaments*, pp. 154–55.

3 James VI and I, 1603-25

James's personality

Despite the concerns that had been expressed throughout much of Elizabeth's reign, when the queen finally died the succession was in fact resolved far more smoothly than many had feared. The obvious successor was James VI of Scotland who, despite the fact that he was the son of Mary Queen of Scots, was a Protestant and already well established as an able and successful ruler of the northern kingdom. Robert Cecil had been in secret correspondence with him since at least 1601, making plans for the event of Elizabeth's death, and when it came the transition was achieved entirely peacefully. James was proclaimed king (in splendid disregard of Henry VIII's 1544 succession act which had debarred James's great-grandmother, Margaret Tudor, and her descendants from the succession) and journeyed south to England, where he was warmly welcomed. Once again, we need to begin by examining the personality and background of the new monarch, the man who now became king of England as well as Scotland.

The Scottish background

Aged only 13 months, James was crowned king of Scotland on 29 July 1567. It was the culmination of a series of extraordinary events.

The infant king's mother, Mary Queen of Scots, had been six months pregnant when she had witnessed the horrible murder of her secretary, David Rizzio, perpetrated by her jealous husband, Lord Darnley. One account tells of how one of the murderers pressed a pistol into Mary's side, a circumstance which some commentators have cited as an explanation for James's fear of violence. Mary was determined upon revenge and it seems likely that she was an accomplice to the murder of her husband, not least because she married the man who undertook the deed, the earl of Bothwell. Having compromised her position in this way, she was obliged to abdicate in 1567 in favour of her son. Thereafter she took refuge in England, where her apparent involvement in a number of plots against Elizabeth culminated in her execution in 1587.

For about 17 years government of Scotland was undertaken on James's behalf by regents, a circumstance that induced severe political instability as various factions plotted and counter-plotted to seize the person of the king. Yet, having developed a mature political spirit by the late 1580s, James prosecuted effectively his resolve 'to draw his nobility to unity and concord and be known as a universal king, impartial to them all'.[1] Above all, by employing what S. J. Houston has described as a series of 'ingenious manoeuvres' – ensuring that the governing body (the general assembly) of the Scottish kirk met irregularly, paying the expenses of its moderate members and attending in person – James broke the power of the presbyterian extremists and thus managed ultimately to tame the independence of the Scottish church.

Weaknesses of James

The older historiography of James I has insisted that there were various aspects of James's character which proved damaging to the stability of government and that his Scottish experience did not equip him well to govern England.[2]

Certainly James's belief that the English nobles were individually as powerful as their Scottish counterparts seems to have led to a poor management of parliament. Of course, all monarchs used their patronage in order to win favour, but James's generosity with honours ensured that by 1604 nearly every member of the privy council had a peerage and – since these men henceforth sat in the Lords rather than the Commons – the lower chamber was seriously deficient in spokesmen of the crown. In the parliament that met in 1604 the king was represented in the Commons by Mr 'Secondary' Herbert and Sir John Stanhope only, neither of whom possessed any of the skills of effective parliamentarians. In 1605 the situation deteriorated yet further when James elevated his leading adviser, Robert Cecil, to the earldom of Salisbury. 'The absence of any firm guidance from above', notes J. P. Kenyon, 'was particularly disastrous in 1614', the occasion when parliament produced no legislation and was dissolved after two months.[3]

James's Scottish experience also encouraged his financial extravagance for, as he noted at the time of his accession, he felt like 'a poor man wandering about forty years in a wilderness and barren soil and now arrived at the land of promise'.[4] Yet England at the beginning of the seventeenth century was far from being 'a land of promise' and the crown simply did not possess the resources to withstand the 'continual haemorrhage of outletting' effected by James.[5] It was an acknowledged duty of the monarch to reward loyal servants but James's extraordinary profligacy resulted in crippling debt. Indeed, as early as 1608 the crown debt amounted to almost £600,000. The crown therefore sought grants of supply from parliament, but members of parliament, continuing to adhere to the medieval notion that the crown should 'live of its own' during peacetime, proved reluctant to subsidise James's giving. It was a circumstance which encouraged strained relations between James and his parliaments.

Evidence also suggests that the crown–parliament relationship was made yet more difficult because James was not prepared to commit himself to the business of state, preferring instead the thrill of the hunt. For this reason he was absent from some of the important debates on the Great Contract in 1610 and it is generally agreed that some of the difficulties that emerged in the second session of the 1621 parliament were because James, hunting at Royston, was physically distant from the centre of affairs.

It is also impossible to deny that the new king of England brought to the throne a coarseness and rudeness which one historian has called 'a fluorescence of obscenity'.[6] 'God's wounds!' the king exclaimed when he was told that the public were impatient to see him. 'I will pull down my breeches and they will also see my arse!'[7] James did not enhance the dignity of monarchy. It was reported that when out hunting he did not dismount in order to relieve himself and so habitually ended the day in a filthy and stinking condition. Weldon, the author of a character assassination of James in 1650, alleged that the king 'never washed his hands, only rubbed his finger ends slightly with a wet napkin'.[8] By publicly showering his favours upon a succession of male favourites the king provoked a good deal of adverse comment. Contemporary observers recorded how 'the King had a loathsome way of lolling his arms about his favourites' necks and kissing them' in public.[9] Lucy Hutchinson, writing later in the century, described the Jacobean court as having been 'a nursery of lust and intemperance'.[10] Masques and set-piece occasions became excuses for uncontrolled revelry, James's doctor lamenting that the king 'promiscuously drinks beer, ale, Spanish wine, sweet French wine . . . muscatelle and sometimes alicante wine'.[11] When James's brother-in-law, King Christian IV of Denmark, visited England in 1606 the evening witnessed much 'sick and spewing'.[12] In the eyes of Lucy Hutchinson, James thus '[betrayed] the honour, wealth and glory of the nation'.[13] Indeed, 'James's neglect of his image', concludes Christopher Durston, 'should probably be seen as his most serious fault'.[14]

Strengths of James

Nevertheless, James had many very real strengths and abilities, not least of which was a preparedness to challenge established prejudices. He certainly possessed a powerful intelligence and great theological knowledge which he enjoyed parading in formal debate such as on the occasion of the Hampton Court Conference in 1604. He was also a prolific writer. The violence of his *Counterblaste to tobacco* would be as warmly accepted today as his support for bear-baiting would be condemned. This 'schoolmaster of the whole land' also developed a healthy scepticism of witchcraft, a scepticism that he also applied to touching for the King's Evil – a practice based on the belief that the monarch could, by their touch, cure a glandular disease called scrofula.

James's most famous publications are probably his book of instructions for his eldest son, Prince Henry, who died in 1612, *Basilikon doron* (1599), and *The trew law of free monarchies* (1598), in which he expounded the theory of divine right of kings. This was the belief, as he told parliament in a speech on 21 March 1610, that 'kings are not only God's lieutenants upon earth, and sit upon God's throne, but even by God himself they are called Gods'. James has often been criticised by historians for the forthright manner in which he reminded parliament of his divine-right authority. However, the majority of his listeners probably shared his sentiment, especially since James recognised a distinction between 'the state of kings in their first original' and 'the state of settled kings and monarchs that do at this time govern in civil kingdoms', a circumstance in which he was bound by his

Coronation Oath to 'the observation of the fundamental laws of this kingdom'. James also promised to 'rule my actions according to my laws' and acknowledged that the law could only be changed 'by the advice of Parliament'. He specifically stated that 'the King *with his Parliament* here are absolute . . . in making or forming any sort of laws'.[15]

The first British monarch was also possessed of a political vision that was ahead of its time, revealed especially in his scheme for a political and religious union between England and Scotland. James envisaged that there would be one faith, one law and one parliament for the whole of the realm. He told his first English parliament that 'what God hath conjoined, let no man separate. I am the husband and the whole isle is my lawful wife; I am the head and it is my body.'[16]

The death of James

King James died at the age of 59 on 27 March 1625, having survived his wife, Anne of Denmark, by six years. He left two children: a daughter, Elizabeth, known as the 'Winter Queen' after her marriage to Frederick of the Palatinate and his subsequent expulsion from his territories in the Thirty Years' War; and a son aged 25 who became King Charles I.

How has James been treated by historians?

Most historians now agree that James I has had a bad press, based for the large part upon Weldon's picture of a monarch of a 'timorous disposition'; an extravagant, dirty, lazy king – 'the wisest fool in Christendom'.[17] Though Weldon had been dismissed from the Jacobean court and therefore had an axe to grind, his highly biased version of events has coloured much later writing and perpetuated the notion that James was an inadequate king of England.

One reason why historians have proved reluctant to revise the Weldonian account of James is that Weldon's unflattering description of James makes so much easier the task of explaining the occurrence of a series of civil wars in the middle of the seventeenth century. According to S. R. Gardiner, it was James – especially as a result of his experiences as King James VI of Scotland, which Gardiner argued did not suitably equip him to rule as King James I of England – who 'sowed the seeds of revolution and disaster'.[18] In essence, the accession of James in 1603 set England upon the high road to civil war.

Revisionist accounts of the outbreak of the English Civil War, by stressing the absence of an ideological polarisation of political opinion until the very eve of the Civil War, have done much to rescue the reputation of James I. Moreover, the notion that James's experience in Scotland had not suitably equipped him to govern England has also been questioned. In particular, Jenny Wormald, realising that Weldon's remarks upon the character of James I 'have virtually nothing in common with (contemporary) descriptions of James VI', has been prompted to ask whether James VI and I was 'two kings or one'.[19] If James is generally understood as having been an effective king of Scotland then why, as James I of England, should he be considered any less impressive? Perhaps the historiography of James VI and I is misleading. Was James perhaps a less good king of Scotland than historians have suggested? Or, alternatively, was James perhaps a much better king of England than has been suggested?

Historians have generally concluded the latter to be the case. In part this has come about by studying James in the broader context of early-seventeenth-century regimes. In part it is a consequence of historians having adopted a much more cautious approach to the use of hostile descriptions of James I than hitherto. Thus it is now generally recognised that it was not unusual for royalty to be extravagant and to take favourites. Similarly, whatever the monarch's personal appearance and behaviour, few of their subjects would ever have seen them. In any case, as J. P. Kenyon has pointed out, '[James's] son Charles I was handsome, dignified and chaste, but much good it did him'.[20] Finally, Wormald has argued that James's Scottish experience of kingship, rather than equipping him inadequately for his reign as James I, 'may have been a very great advantage', at least in political terms. It was an experience which taught him to empathise with his opponents, occasionally to compromise and soften and never to force the pace of events. 'By trying to transmit his Scottish style of kingship to the English throne', notes Wormald, 'he defused problems within the church and the state, and thereby presided over a kingdom probably more stable than his predecessor had left, and certainly than his successor was to rule'.[21]

Jacobean parliaments, 1604–24

James called four parliaments which met in the years 1604–11, 1614, 1621 and 1624 and sat for a total of only 36 months during his 22-year-long reign.

The main reason for a monarch to call parliament was the expectation that it would provide supply, taxation levied by parliaments. Three parliaments of James duly did so; only the parliament of 1614 provided no supply at all. Yet even the supply offered by the parliaments of 1604–11, 1621 and 1624 proved wholly inadequate in relation to the needs of the crown, amounting to just over £900,000 in total, the equivalent of only 9.28 per cent of total revenue received during the whole of James's reign. Conrad Russell has duly concluded that it is 'hard to see what, in financial terms [the king] stood to gain from calling future Parliaments'.[22]

In contrast, parliament's capacity and willingness to pass legislation was impressive. The five sessions of James's first parliament produced no fewer than 226 acts and, though the parliament of 1621 produced only two, there were over 50 in preparation when it was dissolved. The parliament of 1624 produced 73 acts, prompting Derek Hirst to describe this as 'a testimonial to harmony'.[23]

The parliament of 1604–11

The first of James's parliaments concerned itself with a number of issues, the most important of which were:

- the question of who possessed the ultimate authority to judge disputed election returns;

- a consideration of James's desire for a political union with Scotland;
- whether or not a fundamental reformation of the royal finances should take place.

In 1604 there occurred a fierce argument in the Commons over a disputed election return for Buckinghamshire. After the privy councillor Sir John Fortescue had been defeated by Sir Francis Goodwin, the latter's election was declared invalid by the lord chancellor on the grounds that Goodwin was an outlaw. The lord chancellor duly declared that Fortescue was elected in his place.

This event brought to the fore the question of the government's ability to pack parliament, a means by which it might ultimately threaten the independence of the Commons. Henry Yelverton warned that 'a Chancellor may call a Parliament of what persons he will by this course' and the Commons angrily disputed the outcome, eventually ordering Goodwin to take his seat.[24] Ultimately, however, Goodwin was prevented from taking his seat because James quashed the election and ordered another, thereby providing the mechanism for a sensible, compromise outcome. Thus, as J. P. Kenyon notes, 'James's conduct was more judicious and sensible than it has been made to appear, and such mistakes as he made are to be blamed on the bad advice given him by his law officers'.[25] Recent research has also suggested that the crown was in any case less than enthusiastic about Sir John Fortescue.[26]

The Buckinghamshire election case was the genesis for the Form of Apology and Satisfaction of 1604. The older historiography of this period has represented this document as a milestone on the road to civil war, the first occasion when members of parliament sought some form of constitutional protection of their privileges. However, a closer reading of the Apology indicates that it was more concerned with religious matters and the crown's prerogative rights of wardship and marriage than with great touchstone issues such as freedom of speech. Moreover, the Apology was drawn up by a committee of the Commons and was never adopted by the whole house on the grounds that it was thought too inflammatory. Kenyon concluded that 'the Commons' assertion of their privileges was once thought aggressive [but] it could equally well be regarded as neurotically defensive'.[27] Nevertheless, it was clear that there was the appearance of a mutual distrust between king and Commons.

This distrust was deepened by the failure of parliament to concede legal reality to James's wish for a full political union between Scotland and England, an issue which dominated the parliamentary sessions of 1604 and 1607. English hatred of the Scots, combined with a genuine fear about how the laws of the two countries would be assimilated, meant that the scheme was a dead issue by 1607 – though James had made some progress by piecemeal reform by proclamation, such as the creation of the Union flag in 1606 and the abolition of laws limiting trade, aid and communication across the Anglo-Scottish border in 1607. There is no doubt that James was disappointed by the failure of parliament to implement his wishes, but the episode did not represent a fundamental breakdown in relations, though that would surely have come if James had persisted. Moreover, Jenny Wormald has recently suggested that the union scheme was deliberately presented by James as his main ambition so that other measures, such as the introduction of Scots at court, would appear moderate in comparison.[28]

By the time that this parliament met in 1610 for its fourth session, the most pressing matter was that of royal finances, the crown debt amounting to nearly £600,000 even as early as 1608. Salisbury's plan fundamentally to overhaul the basis of crown finance, known as the Great Contract, represented the most far-sighted attempt at financial reform until 1641. In return for an annual grant of £200,000 and a one-off payment of £600,000, James was to surrender wardship and purveyance. In the summer of 1610 agreement along these lines seems to have been reached. However, when parliament reassembled in November, both parties had had second thoughts. On the one hand, members of parliament were reluctant to subsidise an extravagant king and concerned that such a substantial grant might diminish the likelihood of parliaments being called in the future. Moreover, since wardship and purveyance did not affect all parts of the country equally, some constituencies favoured the status quo. On the other hand, if James relinquished wardship and purveyance, he would lose a significant means of recompensing the political support received from courtiers. Above all, in a time of rampant inflation it was blatantly bad economics to exchange flexible revenues for fixed. For these reasons, practical not ideological, did the Great Contract fail.

The parliament of 1614

James's least successful parliament was that which met in 1614; it produced no legislation and is therefore known as the Addled Parliament. As soon as it assembled on 5 April, the atmosphere was soured by rumours that attempts had been made to pack it by government agents, or 'undertakers'. It seems likely that these rumours were fostered by the Howard faction, headed by Northampton, Suffolk and the royal favourite, Somerset. Having risen to prominence after the dissolution of the previous parliament, this element acknowledged that a new parliament would provide their critics with a platform for an assault upon their newly acquired pre-eminence. It therefore also served their purpose to insinuate that the crown might diminish parliament's role by increasingly exploiting impositions, additional duties on imports which brought in about £70,000 per annum – roughly the same as one parliamentary subsidy by this time. This duly encouraged a debate in which the ability of the crown to exercise its prerogative by levying impositions was questioned, even though this had been affirmed as recently as 1606 in Bate's Case.[29] 'So do our impositions increase in England as it is come to be almost tyrannical government in England', alleged Sir Edwin Sandys.[30] In increasingly chaotic circumstances, James dissolved parliament. He angrily informed the Spanish ambassador, 'I am surprised that my ancestors should ever have permitted such an institution to come into existence', though he added 'I am obliged to put up with what I cannot get rid of'.[31] Clearly it was not on James's agenda to rule without parliament on a permanent basis.

The parliament of 1621

After the dissolution of the Addled Parliament, James embarked on a seven-year period of personal rule, attempting to finance his government and personal expenditure through involvement in a disastrous scheme involving trade in cloth – the Cockayne Project – as well as exploiting various fiscal feudal devices such as wardship and purveyance and collecting impositions which he claimed to levy according to his prerogative authority. However, his continued extravagance and the onset of European war from 1618 necessitated that he meet with his third parliament of the reign. A deepening mistrust of Buckingham, the royal favourite since the fall of Somerset in 1615, and the onset of perhaps the worst economic depression of the seventeenth century did not augur well.

Nevertheless, the first session proved a success. Members of parliament studiously avoided a discussion of impositions and instead quickly voted James two subsidies. Moreover, since they held out the prospect of further grants, they immeasurably strengthened James's strategy in his foreign policy; that is, to use parliament as a sabre-rattling device in the hope that it would make enough noise to persuade the Habsburgs to restore Frederick and Elizabeth to the Palatinate. In return James did not prevent members of parliament from investigating royal grants of patents and monopolies, an outcome of which was the revival of the medieval process of impeachment – a trial in parliament in which the Commons acted as prosecutors and the Lords as judges. In the first instance it was used against the monopolists Sir Francis Michell and Sir Giles Mompesson.

The revival of impeachment was once seen as an example of the Commons attempting to limit the power of the crown, especially when it was deployed by this parliament to remove the lord chancellor, Sir Francis Bacon, on the grounds that he had corruptly accepted bribes from Chancery litigants. However, it is now clear that proceedings against Bacon were instigated by his court rivals, Sir Edward Coke and Lionel Cranfield (later made earl of Middlesex), not by the lower house. In any case, members of parliament had reason to be grateful to James, for he seemed genuinely sympathetic to their grievances and during the recess issued a proclamation cancelling 18 monopolies and allowing 17 more to be challenged at common law. Just like Elizabeth, James knew when to make a timely concession in relation to this grievance. The only sour note in relations had been struck when James had ordered the temporary imprisonment during the recess of Southampton, Sandys and Oxford on grounds that they had sought to orchestrate attacks upon Buckingham. It is worth noting that by imprisoning these members during the parliamentary recess, James avoided violating the parliamentary privilege of freedom from arrest while parliament was sitting. Verbally he claimed to have the right to arrest even when parliament was in session, but wisely – unlike Charles I – he never put this to the test in practice.

The second session lasted no more than four weeks and ended acrimoniously in the most extraordinary scene from all James's parliaments. With the Palatinate question still unresolved, and with no direction from the government, members of parliament claimed the right to discuss foreign policy, a key aspect of the

Reynold Elstrack's engraving of James I in parliament. James is surrounded by his English privy councillors, and on his left is Prince Charles.

prerogative. They duly exhorted James 'speedily and effectually to take the sword into your hand' and requested that 'our most noble prince [i.e. Charles] may be timely and happily married to one of our own religion', thus going directly against James's policy of marrying Charles to the infanta – the Spanish Match.[32] When James forbade them to discuss these matters, an agitated Commons produced a protestation in which they propounded their belief that freedom of speech amounted to their 'ancient and undoubted birthright'.[33] Shortly afterwards James tore the Protestation from the journal of the house and then dissolved parliament. Yet this was certainly not the inevitable outcome of a relationship between crown and parliament which had been steadily deteriorating since 1603. Indeed, it is difficult to see this as anything more than a temporary aberration in the operation of the machinery of state – a view which is substantiated by the history of the parliament of 1624.

The parliament of 1624

In 1624, with the Palatinate crisis no nearer solution, James called his final, and in many ways most successful, parliament.

45

The success of this parliament was largely a result of the machinations of Charles and Buckingham. Embittered by the failure of their trip to Spain in 1623 (Charles had imagined himself in love with the infanta), the heir and the favourite returned to England determined upon war. In order to dispel memories of the free-speech debacle of 1621, Buckingham persuaded James to make an opening address in which the king invited the houses to proffer 'advice in the greatest matters that ever could concern any king; a greater declaration of my confidence in you I cannot give'.[34] Charles and Buckingham then gave assurances that money granted by parliament would be spent in ways which the Commons approved, namely a war against Spain. Thus, an appropriation clause to this effect was inserted into the 1624 subsidy act. Ultimately, the parliament of 1624 produced 73 statutes – notable amongst which was the Monopolies Act, declaring grants of monopolies to individuals illegal.

The older historiography of this period held that the appropriation clause was devised by the Commons and as such was something of a constitutional landmark in the development of a 'limited monarchy'. However, since recent research has demonstrated that it originated at court, this can no longer be held to be the case. Moreover, it is now also clear that it was Buckingham and Charles who orchestrated at this time the impeachment of Lord Treasurer Middlesex on the grounds that he opposed the war effort. Once again, an event which was previously interpreted as the Commons 'winning the initiative' *vis-à-vis* the crown has been fundamentally reassessed. Similarly, it has been noted that the Monopolies Act was left sufficiently vague to allow the monarch to continue making monopoly grants, though henceforth only to companies.

However, in one respect James's final parliament did sound an ominous note. Whereas most of the Jacobean parliaments had remained free of religious controversy, the parliament of 1624 submitted a complaint against Richard Montagu's *A new gag for an old goose*, a tract which argued that the points of difference between the churches of Rome and England were far fewer than had been supposed. James treated the complaint with disdain but it provided a warning for the future.

A limited monarchy?

The older historiography of this period argued that parliament, in order to resist what were seen as the autocratic tendencies of James I, increasingly circum-scribed the crown prerogative. It was, in other words, 'winning the initiative'.[35] According to this argument, parliament withheld supply in order to coerce the crown into redressing the grievances of the political nation (and their represent-atives) and developed procedural devices, such as the Committee of the Whole House, which enabled members of the Commons to circumvent restrictions imposed by a pro-government speaker. These so-called Whig historians also argued that the Commons sought their objectives not only by coercing, but also by invading, the royal prerogative – in particular in the way that impeachment was revived in order to remove royal councillors and through the attachment of the appropriation clauses to the Subsidy Act in 1624. All of this certainly seems to suggest that by 1625 the power of the English monarchy was limited in relation to what it had been in 1603.

However, the argument put forward by the Whigs has been significantly diminished by a number of revisionist historians.[36] They have demonstrated not only the absence of any continuity of opposition in the Jacobean parliaments, but also that when opposition did appear it was not ideologically inspired. They acknowledge that there were disputes centred on the perceived privileges of members of parliament against the prerogative of the crown, but point out that these were no more intense – and perhaps even less so – than in previous parliaments. Indeed, it is now clear that those occasions which had previously been understood as milestones on the road to a limited monarchy were instead the result of factions in the Commons and the Lords temporarily collaborating in order to achieve a particular goal – the impeachment of a minister or the attachment of clauses to the 1624 subsidy bill, for example. Members of parliament were thus not bent upon diminishing the crown's prerogative any more than they had been under Elizabeth. Above all, with the monarch retaining the prerogative ability to call, prorogue and dissolve parliaments, the 'initiative' remained with the crown. Indeed, pointing to the effect of inflation upon the value of a subsidy – diminishing from around £70,000 in 1603 to £55,000 by the mid-1620s – the revisionists have highlighted the fundamental weakness of parliament, that it was increasingly reluctant to grant subsidies of diminishing value. In this sense what is surprising is not that James called as many parliaments as he did but that he called them at all.

Religion and the church, 1603–25

In 1603 James inherited an English church settlement which had been fashioned by Elizabeth in 1559, the famous middle way or *via media*. In essence, this had retained the Catholic structure of the church – a hierarchical edifice staffed by bishops and archbishops, though the head of the church in England was now the monarch – whilst replacing the celebration of mass with a Protestant ceremony which emphasised the merely symbolic significance of the bread and the wine. At the start of the seventeenth century there were signs that this compromise was beginning to be challenged from both ends of the religious spectrum, the Catholics on the one hand and the Puritans, the 'hotter form of Protestant', on the other. In 1603 each looked to James with high hopes that he would remedy their grievances. It was an uneasy circumstance.

Yet, only during the years 1603–6 and again from 1618 is it possible to perceive religion as a threat to the stability of the Jacobean regime. It is a testament to the vision and even-handedness of James that the fraying of the Elizabethan *via media* did not develop into a dangerously destabilising process of polarisation during his reign, not least because this very process was taking place on the continent.

The fashioning of a new *via media*, 1603–6

The Puritans

The Puritans had reason to be hopeful that the new king would complete the processes of reformation which they had felt were compromised by the Elizabethan church settlement. Indeed, James had already made known his desire to halt the plundering of the church and to raise the standards of the ministry. Furthermore, he appeared a committed Calvinist who had declared in his book *Basilikon doron* that he was indifferent to what he called the 'outward badges of popish errors' such as the wearing by ministers of the surplice and hood.[37] However, whilst the moderate Puritans wanted no more than the abolition of popish 'outward badges', their brethren – the 'hottest' form of Puritans, known as Presbyterians – were opposed to the fundamentals of episcopal government of the church.

It was the demands of the moderate Puritans that found their way into the Millenary Petition, a document supposedly carrying a thousand signatures and presented to the king in April 1603. The signatories sought to be 'eased and relieved' of those ceremonies and practices which they considered to be remnants of the popish church.[38] These included:

- the use of the cross in baptism;
- the use of the ring in marriage;
- bowing at the name of Jesus;
- confirmation;
- the administration of baptism by women;
- the wearing of the surplice and hood.

They also demanded:

- that the ministry be staffed by able and sufficient men;
- that ministers be properly maintained;
- that an end be put to pluralism.

This was an extensive set of reform proposals but it was also studiously moderate. Above all, the demand that episcopacy be abolished or removed was noticeable by its absence. The king, always keen to engage in theological debate, duly agreed to convene at Hampton Court in January 1604 a conference to discuss the requests put forward in the Millenary Petition.

The Hampton Court Conference, January 1604

Along with Archbishop Whitgift, eight bishops were selected to attend at Hampton Court, including the anti-Puritan Richard Bancroft, shortly to be appointed archbishop of Canterbury. The representatives of the Puritans were led by John Reynolds, president of Corpus Christi College, Oxford. When Reynolds mentioned 'presbytery', James made it immediately clear that he regarded those who wished to abolish bishops and establish a presbyterian model along Scottish lines as subversive radicals. 'A Scottish presbytery agreeth as well with monarchy as God and the Devil', he exclaimed. He proceeded to inform his listeners that 'I know what would become of my supremacy: no bishop, no king.'[39] Thus, he believed that if the institution of episcopacy was abolished then the authority of the crown would be fatally weakened.

The older historiography of this royal eruption suggests that this was the point at which the Puritans became an irreconcilable, dangerously subversive element who eventually obtained their goals by force in the 'Puritan Revolution' of 1642. Yet James quickly proceeded to offer a number of concessions designed to appease the moderate Puritans, including a promise to enhance endowments in order to improve the quality of the clergy, reduce pluralism and non-residence and commission a new translation of the Bible, the famous Authorised Version of 1611. These concessions, as Kenneth Fincham and Peter Lake have noted, '[were intended] to settle the issue of Puritanism once and for all by driving a wedge between the moderate and radical wings of Puritan opinion. The moderates were to be fully and finally integrated into the national church, while the extremists were to be expelled or repressed.'[40]

As a means 'to discern the affections of persons, whether quiet or turbulent', clergy were formally to accept the Canons of 1604, the most important of which for James's purpose was Canon 36.[41] Each minister was to subscribe – append his name – to each of the three articles of this Canon, which duly bound him to:

- recognise James as the 'only supreme governor' of an episcopalian church;
- accept that there was 'nothing contrary to the Word of God' in the Book of Common Prayer;
- 'acknowledgeth all' of the Thirty-Nine Articles, the established beliefs of the Church of England.

It followed, therefore, that once a minister had subscribed to Canon 36, he effectively 'renounced subversive disobedience to the royal command'.[42] Any minister who refused to subscribe was to be deprived of his benefice, the effect of which was to distinguish the moderate Puritans from the more hardline Presbyterians and generally to weaken, by splitting, the reform cause. Most Puritans were clearly prepared to accept the reforms offered at Hampton Court in exchange for conformity with the established church; by the end of 1604 only 73–83 beneficed clergy out of a total of around 9,000 were deprived. The king's scheme proved especially durable because, once a minister had formally recognised James as head of the church and accepted that the institution of episcopacy was unalterable, James was prepared to turn a blind eye to any minister who did not comply with ceremonial practices such as the wearing of the surplice and hood. By this means, observe Fincham and Lake, 'moderate Puritans who held misgivings about aspects of the rites and discipline of the church were accommodated within it since they posed no threat to the stability of church or state'.[43] For these reasons Frederick Shriver has concluded that the Hampton Court Conference was 'one of the most significant events in the political and religious history of England'.[44]

The nature of the episcopal bench
In his determination to give the church as broad a base of support as possible, James promoted a wide range of opinions in his appointments of bishops. Intent

upon a policy of tolerance towards the moderate episcopalian Puritans, James appointed George Abbot as archbishop of Canterbury in 1611, thus providing a suitable contrast to his predecessor, Richard Bancroft. Indeed, between 1611 and 1625 only two ministers were deprived for nonconformity. The bench of bishops as a whole represented a diversity of opinion, upon which sat on the one hand staunch Calvinists like Toby Matthew, archbishop of York, and John King, bishop of London; and on the other anti-Calvinists like Richard Neile, Lancelot Andrewes and William Laud. In between stood a range of moderate opinion.

The Catholics

In 1603 the Catholics had reason to hope that they would be treated rather more leniently by James than by his Protestant predecessors. After all, James was the son of the Catholic Mary Queen of Scots and himself married to a Catholic queen, Anne of Denmark. Moreover, when the Catholic earl of Northumberland had suggested to James that it would be 'a pity to lose so good a kingdom [i.e. England] for not tolerating a mass in the corner', the king had responded by saying, 'I will neither persecute any that will be quiet and give but an outward obedience to the law', the very approach he was to take in relation to the problem of Protestant nonconformity.[45]

Yet for a number of reasons Catholic ambitions came to nothing. In particular, members of parliament demanded that repressive measures once more be taken against the Catholics when the details of the Bye Plot were revealed, a scheme devised by William Watson to kidnap the king and force him to implement an earlier promise of toleration for Catholics. Moreover, there remained a persistent fear that Spain was determined to establish a 'universal monarchy' despite the conclusion of the Anglo-Spanish war in November 1604. Feeling embittered and betrayed, an extremist group led by Robert Catesby sought to blow up the king, the queen, Prince Henry, bishops, nobles, councillors, judges, knights and burgesses. Yet not even the discovery of the Gunpowder Plot deflected James from his central belief that 'as long as the Catholics remain quiet and decently hidden they will neither be hunted nor persecuted'.[46]

In order to distinguish those 'factious stirrers of sedition' from those who sought to 'remain quiet and decently hidden', James imposed an oath of allegiance upon all Catholics in 1606.[47] Those who took the oath agreed not only that 'James is the lawful and rightful king' but also that the papal power of excommunication was a 'damnable doctrine'.[48] As in his treatment of the Puritans, the king thus placed priority upon political allegiance to himself and the national church and played down the question of doctrinal and ceremonial conformity. As James stated,[49] his intention was:

> to make a separation between so many of my subjects, who although they were popishly affected, yet retained in their hearts the print of their natural duty to their sovereign; and those who . . . thought diversity of religion a safe pretext for all kinds of treasons and rebellions against their sovereign.

A quest for a British church

Having styled himself 'King of Great Britain' by a proclamation of October 1604, it is not surprising that James sought to bring the churches of England, Scotland and Ireland into closer 'congruity' with each other.[50] He did not intend to impose a uniformity upon the three kingdoms but he did seek to diminish the differences that continued to exist between the three national Protestant churches. Thus the Irish Articles of 1615 were modelled directly on the English Calvinist Articles of 1595, though they were of limited impact since the overwhelming majority of the Irish population remained Catholic. In Scotland, by means of piecemeal reform, James succeeded in inserting episcopacy into the Presbyterian church – an extraordinary achievement by any standards. He also secured a successful passage for the Five Articles of Perth through both the general assembly of the Scottish kirk in 1618 and the Scottish parliament in 1621. Since they required the Scots, amongst other things, to observe the saints' days as recognised by the English church and to kneel at communion, they unsurprisingly proved highly contentious and extremely difficult to enforce. Yet they none the less diminished a potential cause of Anglo-Scottish dissension because, as Conrad Russell points out, 'a Scot who had subscribed to the Five Articles of Perth might never kneel again, but he could no longer condemn the English for doing so without condemning himself as a perjurer'.[51]

The breakdown of the Jacobean compromise

Christopher Durston has recently concluded that the religious equilibrium established by James meant that 'the English Church enjoyed more tranquillity than at any time since the Reformation'.[52] Similarly, J. P. Kenyon regarded James's religious *via media* as his 'finest achievement, . . . a religious detente which had entirely eluded Elizabeth'. However, this equilibrium, so finely fashioned, was not particularly stable. From about 1618 it began to break down.

One reason for this development may have been because as James grew older he seems to have developed real doubts about the Calvinist theory of predestination, perhaps most notoriously signalled by his allowing the publication in 1624 of Richard Montagu's *A new gag for an old goose*. In this tract Montagu proceeded to attack the Calvinist belief that God alone determined whether a soul would go to heaven or hell, an opinion which James angrily defended by exclaiming 'if this be popery I am a papist'.[53] Already, in 1618, James had issued the Book of Sports, permitting people to participate in a large number of recreations on a Sunday. It may well have been that James was acting with the best of intentions because, as he had passed through Lancashire upon his return from Scotland in 1617, he had been made aware of a general resentment of Calvinist attempts to ban recreation on a Sunday – so great in fact that some were adopting Catholicism. But the notion that Sundays should be set aside for worship was so fundamental to Calvinist belief that many regarded the Book of Sports with horror.

In fact James's Calvinist credentials remained intact, evidenced by his sending of representatives to the Synod of Dort in 1618 in order to condemn the views of

Jacobus Arminius, a champion of the anti-Calvinists.[54] It was Jacobean foreign policy that created circumstances in which it became increasingly difficult to maintain the religious consensus. For complex personal and political reasons, James sought to marry his son to a Spanish Catholic. The so-called Spanish Match, always unpopular amongst the majority of the political nation – not least because it led to the lenient treatment of English Catholics – became widely and deeply resented after the outbreak of the Thirty Years' War in 1618 and the consequent advance of Catholic interests on the continent. The very success of the Catholic powers sharpened Calvinist attacks upon James's leniency towards the English Catholics and his foreign policy in general, a development which the king tried to counter by formally gagging criticism of royal policy in his Directions to Preachers (1622) and by promoting anti-Calvinists. This polarisation was potentially dangerously destabilising, though it was not actually to become so until the accession of Charles I.

The situation in 1625

Although it had experienced assaults upon its authority from both ends of the religious spectrum, the crown was by no means weakened. Indeed, the effect of some of these assaults, especially the Gunpowder Plot, enhanced the authority of the crown – so obviously that some historians have questioned whether the whole affair was devised by Salisbury. Members of the political nation, having stared into the abyss and foreseen a fearful breakdown in law and order, were eager to bolster the authority of the crown. For example, in the immediate aftermath of the discovery of the plot, Sir Edward Hexter moved that the speaker of the house 'should make manifest the thankfulness of the House to God, for [the king's] safe deliverance' and that 'they would all, and every one of them, be ready [to support him] with the uttermost Drop of their Blood'.[55] More than ever, members of parliament saw it as absolutely necessary to support a Protestant king in order to overcome the forces of darkness.

The threat from the other end of the religious spectrum, largely imperceptible after 1604, became more pointed after 1618. Yet it never seriously threatened the continued existence of the institution of episcopacy and the crown's ability to nominate its members, a fundamental aspect of royal authority.

Document case study

Parliamentary 'opposition' to the monarchy

3.1 The Venetian ambassador's letter to the doge and senate of Venice, 28 April 1604

On Monday the question of the union of England and Scotland came up. The King greatly desires it, but various . . . points are sustained and argued by both sides with such heat that the King doubts whether he will be able to surmount the difficulties.

Source: *Calendar of state papers Venetian*, vol. 10, p. 148.

3.2 The king's letter to the privy council, 7 December 1610

[We] are sure no House save the House of Hell could have found so many [complaints] as they have already done . . . [We] are sorry of our ill fortune in this country . . . Wherein we have misbehaved ourself here we know not, nor can we never yet learn . . . Our fame and actions have been daily tossed like tennis balls amongst them and all that spite and malice durst do to disgrace . . . us hath been used. To be short, this Lower House by their behaviour have imperilled and annoyed our health, wounded our reputation, emboldened all ill-natured people, encroached upon many of our privileges, and plagued our purse with their delays.

Source: G. P. V. Akrigg (ed.), *The letters of King James VI and I*, London, 1984, pp. 318–19.

3.3 James's response to a petition from the Commons, 11 December 1621

In the body of your petition you usurp upon our prerogative royal, and meddle with things far above your reach, and then in the conclusion you protest the contrary; as if a robber would take a man's purse and then protest he meant not to rob him. For first, you presume to give us your advice concerning the match of our dearest son with some Protestant . . . princess . . . and dissuade us from his match with Spain, urging us to a present war with that King; and yet in the conclusion, forsooth, ye protest ye intend not to press upon our most undoubted and regal prerogative . . .

And although we cannot allow of the style, [your] calling it [i.e. privileges claimed by members of parliament, especially freedom of speech and freedom from arrest whilst parliament is in session] 'your ancient and undoubted right and inheritance' . . . yet we are pleased to give you our royal assurance that as long as you contain yourselves within the limits of your duty, we will be as careful to maintain and preserve your lawful liberties and privileges as ever any of our predecessors . . . So as your House shall only have need to beware to trench upon the prerogative of the crown which would enforce us, or any just king, to retrench them of their privileges that would pare his prerogative and flowers of the Crown . . .

Source: John Rushworth (ed.), *Historical collections of private passages of state*, 8 vols., London, 1659–1701, vol. 1, pp. 46–52, reprinted in J. R. Tanner (ed.), *Constitutional documents of James I*, Cambridge, 1930, pp. 283–87.

3.4 James's response to the parliament of 1624

I will deal frankly with you: show me the means how I may do what you would have of me, and if I take a resolution by your advice to enter into a war, then yourselves by your own deputies shall have the disposing of the money . . . I say this with a purpose to invite you to open your purses . . . If upon your offer I shall find the means to make the war honourable and safe, and that I promise you in the word of a King, that although war and peace be peculiar prerogatives of kings, yet, as I have advised with you in the Treaties on which war may ensue, so I will not treat nor accept of a Peace, without first acquainting you with it.

Source: *Lords' journals*, vol. 3, pp. 250–51, reprinted in Tanner (ed.), *Constitutional documents of James I*, pp. 298–99.

3.5 The Subsidy Act, 1624

And . . . be it further enacted, that as well the said treasurers as the said persons appointed for the Council of War as aforesaid, and all other persons who shall be trusted with the receiving, issuing, bestowing, and employing of these moneys or any part thereof . . . shall be answerable and accountable for their doings or proceedings herein to the Commons in Parliament.

Source: 21 & 22 Jac. I, c. 33: *Statutes of the realm*, vol. 4, p. 1247, reprinted in Tanner (ed.), *Constitutional documents of James I*, p. 377.

Document case-study questions

1 What evidence is there in these documents that the Commons had 'encroached upon many [royal] privileges' by 1625?

2 What can be inferred from document 3.3 about the Commons' complaints? Assess the effectiveness of James's response.

3 Considering the tone of and content of 3.1, 3.2 and 3.3, to what extent are you surprised by James's statement in 3.4? Use your knowledge of the period to offer a full explanation.

Notes and references

1 Quoted in David Harris Willson, *King James VI and I*, London, 1963, p. 47.

2 Perhaps the most damning of these is Willson, *King James VI and I*.

3 J. P. Kenyon, *The Stuarts*, Glasgow, 1958, p. 47.

4 Quoted in Willson, *King James VI and I*, p. 171.

5 Quoted in A. Somerset, *Unnatural murder: poison at the court of James I*, London, 1998, p. 40.

6 D. H. Willson, *King James VI and I*, p. 36.

7 As recorded by Sir John Oglander, *A royalist's notebook*, in Irene Carrier (ed.), *King James VI and I*, Cambridge, 1998, p. 12.

8 Weldon's account can be found in Carrier (ed.), *King James VI and I*, p. 9.

9 Quoted in Somerset, *Unnatural murder*, p. 59.

10 Lucy Hutchinson, *Memoirs of the life of Colonel Hutchinson*, London, 1995, p. 62.

11 Quoted in Willson, *King James VI and I*, p. 194.

12 Quoted in Willson, *King James VI and I*, p. 194.

13 Hutchinson, *Memoirs*, p. 62.

14 Christopher Durston, *James I*, London, 1993, p. 12.

15 For this speech see J. P. Kenyon (ed.), *The Stuart Constitution: documents and commentary*, 2nd edition, Cambridge, 1986, pp. 11–12.

16 For this speech, see Carrier (ed.), *James VI and I*, p. 31.

17 See note 8, above.

18 S. R. Gardiner, *History of England 1603–1642*, London, 1883, vol. 5, p. 316.

19 Jenny Wormald, 'James VI and I: two kings or one?', *History*, 68 (1983), pp. 187–209 (quotation at p. 191).

20 J. P. Kenyon, *Stuart England*, London, 1978, p. 50.

21 See Wormald, 'Two kings or one?', pp. 208–9.

22 Conrad Russell, *Parliaments and English politics 1621–1629*, Oxford, 1979, p. 53.

23 Derek Hirst, *Authority and conflict: England 1603–1658*, London, 1986, p. 135.

24 Quoted in Roger Lockyer, *The early Stuarts: a political history of England 1603–1642*, Harlow, 1998, p. 103.

25 Kenyon (ed.), *Stuart Constitution*, p. 25.

26 R. C. Munden, 'The defeat of Sir John Fortescue: court versus country at the hustings', *English Historical Review*, 93 (1978), pp. 811–16.

27 Kenyon (ed.), *Stuart Constitution*, p. 25.

28 See Jenny Wormald, 'James VI, James I and the identity of Britain', in Brendan Bradshaw and John Morrill (eds.), *The British problem, c. 1534–1707: state formation in the Atlantic archipelago*, London, 1996, pp. 148–71.

29 In 1606 John Bate refused to pay impositions on currants imported from the eastern Mediterranean, insisting that he was under no obligation to do so since they had not received parliament's consent. Bate was duly sued in the Court of Exchequer, where the judges upheld the king's right to levy impositions. They ruled that this fell within his 'absolute prerogative' (which operated outside but not contrary to the law) rather than his legal prerogative. In other words, the regulation of trade was deemed to be among those emergency powers through which the crown controlled foreign policy.

30 Quoted in David L. Smith, *A history of the modern British Isles, 1603–1707: the double crown*, Oxford, 1998, p. 35.

31 Quoted in Gardiner, *History*, vol. 2, p. 251.

32 See Kenyon (ed.), *Stuart Constitution*, pp. 39–42.

33 See Kenyon (ed.), *Stuart Constitution*, pp. 42–43.

34 See Kenyon (ed.), *Stuart Constitution*, p. 43.

35 See Wallace Notestein, 'The winning of the initiative by the House of Commons', *Proceedings of the British Academy*, 11 (1924–25), pp. 125–75.

36 For examples of revisionists, and a summary of their position, see Glenn Burgess, 'On revisionism: an analysis of early Stuart historiography in the 1970s and 1980s', in *Historical Journal*, 33 (1990), pp. 609–27.

37 Johann P. Sommerville (ed.), *King James VI and I, political writings*, Cambridge, 1994, p. 7.

38 The Millenary Petition is in Kenyon (ed.), *Stuart Constitution*, pp. 114–19.

39 These phrases are quoted in Willson, *King James VI and I*, p. 207.

40 Kenneth Fincham and Peter Lake, 'The ecclesiastical policy of King James I', *Journal of British Studies*, 24 (1985), pp. 171–72.

41 Quoted in S. J. Houston, *James I*, 2nd edition, Harlow, 1995, p. 59.

42 The Canons are in Kenyon (ed.), *Stuart Constitution*, pp. 122–26.

43 Fincham and Lake, 'Ecclesiastical policy', p. 179.

44 Frederick Shriver, 'Hampton Court re-visited: James I and the Puritans', *Journal of Ecclesiastical History*, 33 (1982), quotation at p. 48.

45 Quoted in Willson, *James VI and I*, pp. 148–49.

46 Quoted in Fincham and Lake, 'Ecclesiastical policy', p. 184.

47 Quoted in Fincham and Lake, 'Ecclesiastical policy', p. 184.

48 The oath can be found in Alan Dures, *English Catholicism 1558–1642*, Harlow, 1983, pp. 98–99.

49 Quoted in Kenneth Fincham and Peter Lake, 'The ecclesiastical policies of James I and Charles I', in Kenneth Fincham (ed.), *The early Stuart church, 1603–1642*, London, 1993, p. 29.

50 John Morrill, 'A British patriarchy? Ecclesiastical imperialism under the early Stuarts', in Anthony Fletcher and Peter Roberts (eds.), *Religion, culture and society in early modern Britain: essays in honour of Patrick Collinson*, Cambridge, 1994, pp. 209–37.

51 Conrad Russell, *The causes of the English Civil War*, Oxford, 1990, p. 49.

52 Christopher Durston, *James I*, p. 58.

53 Quoted in David L. Smith, *The Stuart parliaments, 1603–1689*, London, 1999, p. 112.

54 So much so that the anti-Calvinists are usually termed 'Arminians'.

55 Quoted in Antonia Fraser, *The Gunpowder Plot: terror and faith in 1605*, London, 1997, pp. 192–93.

4 Charles I and Oliver Cromwell, 1625–60

The personalities of Charles I and Oliver Cromwell

Charles I

In a number of ways Charles I was not an unattractive personality. After the assassination of Buckingham in 1628 the king fell in love with his French Catholic wife, Henrietta Maria, and subsequently proved to be a loyal husband and a devoted father to his nine children. He was also concerned with the fate of his exiled sister Elizabeth, the 'Winter Queen'. During the calm of the 1630s he built up one of the most impressive art collections in Europe and became something of an authority on the subject. Charles also became a great patron of poetry, plays and masques. He did not indulge his own interests at the expense of the demands of government, for he approached his duties with an energy and conscientiousness which had been absent from his father's reign. During the troubles of the 1640s he proved himself to be physically courageous, and at the Battle of Naseby he had to be prevented from jeopardising his personal safety.

Despite these qualities, most historians are now agreed that, in the words of L. J. Reeve, Charles I 'was not, by inclination or equipment, a political man'.[1] Indeed, one historian has concluded that he was 'unfit to be King'.[2]

Unfit to be king?

Charles was possessed of a self-righteousness, an unctuous rectitude which is manifest in the proclamation he issued after the collapse of his third parliament in 1629:

> we shall be more inclinable to meet in parliament again when our people shall see more clearly into our intentions and actions [and] when such as have bred this interruption [of parliaments] shall have received their condign punishment, and those who are misled by them and by such ill reports as are raised upon this occasion shall come to a better understanding of us and themselves.[3]

This aspect of the royal personality had important political ramifications. Firstly, it meant that Charles was peculiarly obstructive and that his political style was confrontational. Secondly, it led him to define previously existing grey areas on his terms. This was particularly significant for the church because Charles's promotion of the anti-Calvinists at the expense of other opinion resulted in a dangerous process of polarisation.

Charles's inflexibility was stiffened by the fact that he regarded any criticism of royal policies as a personal attack, leading one historian to conclude that Charles was 'in the grip of something approaching paranoia'.[4] It is highly characteristic of Charles that he felt that problems could be solved by removing individuals from parliament – as he did in 1626 and attempted to do in 1642 – rather than by addressing those issues which had caused concern.

When Charles was obliged to offer concessions, they were often accompanied with such ill-grace that they raised concern as to how far the king could be trusted – an early example being Charles's behaviour over the Petition of Right in 1628, including the order that the statute number originally assigned to the petition be removed with a pumice stone in order to make its authority as a statute much less certain. Confirmation that the king could not be trusted was provided by his implication in the Army Plots and 'Incident' of 1641. These events help to explain why there was no settlement during this period because parliament was henceforth encouraged to demand limitations upon the royal prerogative, limitations which proved unacceptable to Charles's notion of divinely ordained monarchy. The king's attempts to play off his opponents after the first Civil War, apparently proceeding to settle with one whilst simultan-eously forming a military alliance with another, were directly responsible for parliament's passing the Vote of No Addresses in January 1648. Though many members of parliament were prepared to soften their position after the defeat of the king in the second Civil War, this was not the case as far as the army was concerned. Having declared Charles a 'man of blood', they purged parliament on 6 December 1648 of all those who had voted to continue negotiations with the king, an event which led directly to the regicide. A knowledge of the duplicitous nature of Charles is thus central to understanding the key moments of his reign.

Oliver Cromwell

Like Charles I, Oliver was a committed family man. He married Elizabeth Bourchier in 1620 and they had a total of eight children. It is not true that Oliver was the archetypal puritan kill-joy. Even James Heath, in his hostile Restoration biography, acknowledged that Cromwell 'was a great lover of music and entertained the most skilful in that science in his pay and family . . . Generally he respected a love to all ingenious and eximious [= choice] persons in any arts, whom he arranged to be sent or brought to him'.[5] As Barry Coward has noted, '[Cromwell's] patronage and employment of artists, poets and dramatists is well-attested enough to despatch the image of Cromwell the cultural philistine to the historical dustbin'.[6]

Cromwell was also a deeply godly man, his victories on the field of battle convincing him that God was on his side, that success had been brought about by 'the great hand of God'.[7] In particular, Cromwell felt certain that God approved of his desire to provide liberty to all Protestant consciences. Yet this ambition proved inconsistent with his other main aim, which came to the fore after the killing of the king in 1649: a determination to found republican government upon consent rather than coercion. Necessary for settled government were freely elected parliaments, but opinion in such parliaments was likely to be antagonistic to the notion of providing for a form of religious toleration because of the latter's association with a breakdown in law and order. In a neat phrase, Blair Worden has thus diagnosed Cromwell as having suffered from 'ideological schizophrenia'.[8]

This does much to explain Oliver's impetuosity and resort to heavy-handed measures in the 1650s which, coupled with his failure to present his parliaments with a programme, contributed to the short-lived nature of the republican experiment.

Parliaments and politics, 1625–60

1625–29 and 1640

During the first four years of his reign Charles called three parliaments. After an 11-year interval from 1629, he then called another parliament in 1640, known as the Short Parliament.

Charles's main reason for calling parliaments in the 1620s was the expectation that they would vote supply for the wars against Spain and, from 1626, France also. However, these parliaments failed to provide sufficient money in order to prosecute the wars successfully and by 1629 relations between the crown and the political nation had deteriorated significantly from what they had been in 1625. This is explained by three factors in particular: religious developments; Buckingham and his association with military failure; and the inflexible, duplicitous character of Charles.

Uncertain about what sort of war they were being asked to support, members of parliament voted only two subsidies in 1625. They also broke with tradition by voting tonnage and poundage to Charles for only one year instead of for life. Thereafter, in noticeable contrast to the Jacobean parliaments, they spent much of their time discussing religion, especially the case of Montagu (see p. 51). In an extraordinarily provocative move, Charles duly appointed Montagu a royal chaplain. The houses responded by drawing up a petition to Charles in which they complained of the recent 'animating of the popish party' and urged, amongst other things, an enforcement of the recusancy laws. Regarding this as an invasion of his prerogative, Charles dissolved parliament.

As lord admiral, Buckingham was made the scapegoat for the disastrous Cadiz expedition in the autumn of 1625. Anticipating an attack upon his favourite in the parliament he called in 1626, Charles prevented six of the most outspoken members of the previous parliament from sitting by appointing them as sheriffs, a device which meant that they were ineligible for election. He also created a number of new peers in order to enhance his support in the Lords. Despite these preparations, Charles immediately lost control of this parliament. Having voted three subsidies, members made their grant conditional upon the removal of Buckingham – now even more of a grievance since he had demonstrated his attachment to the anti-Calvinists at a meeting with them at York House in early 1626. Increasingly exasperated, Charles prevented those he regarded as spearheading the opposition from sitting: he excluded Arundel and Bristol from the Lords and arrested two members of the Commons, Digges and Eliot. Yet such an action trespassed onto what members of parliament regarded as a key aspect of their privilege and both houses refused to proceed with any business until their members were reinstated. When parliament resumed, the Commons began impeachment proceedings against Buckingham. In order to save his favourite, the king dissolved parliament and proceeded to raise war funds by resorting to prerogative taxation, first of all by demanding a benevolence in 1626 and then by means of a forced loan in 1627.

When Buckingham suffered a humiliating reverse in his attempt to relieve the Protestant colony at La Rochelle in the summer of 1627, Charles was once again obliged to call a parliament in order to seek war funds. It first met in March 1628 in an atmosphere of deepening mistrust of the king, generated especially over the collection of the Forced Loan.

The Forced Loan had raised once again the issue of whether the crown had the right to levy taxation without parliamentary consent. Although it was generally accepted that the crown could raise prerogative taxation in an emergency, there was serious debate as to what circumstances amounted to an 'emergency' and who could declare an emergency. As resistance grew, Charles began to billet soldiers on the poorer of his subjects who refused to pay the loan and imprisoned 'by His Majesty's special commandment' a total of about 70 leading men who failed to pay. Five of these duly challenged the legality of their imprisonment – the celebrated Five Knights' Case. They sought a writ of *habeas corpus*, demanding that they should be granted bail unless a reason was given for their detention. Some members of parliament later claimed that this case suggested that the king was trying to assert his prerogative powers at the expense of the common law. To many observers it seemed that the crown was enhancing its power, and thus Sir Benjamin Rudyerd considered the forthcoming parliament to represent 'the crisis of Parliaments: we shall know by this if Parliaments live or die'.[9]

The Petition of Right in 1628 temporarily diminished the atmosphere of crisis. In return for Charles accepting that non-parliamentary taxation, the imposition of martial law, the billeting of troops on civilians and imprisonment without cause shown were all contrary to the 'laws and statutes of this realm', the Commons confirmed their grant of five subsidies. Disguised as a conservative statement of existing laws, the petition constituted a new limitation on royal powers. It sought to impose constraints upon royal actions in a way not seen under Elizabeth and James. However, when the petition was printed, it was found that it was not accompanied by the traditional form of royal assent associated with a petition but by an evasive form of words of Charles's own making, thus casting real doubt on whether the petition could be invoked in the law courts against royal actions.

It might have been expected that the second session of this parliament would have gone more smoothly than the first because Buckingham, whom members had studiously avoided attacking in order to prevent a peremptory dissolution, was assassinated whilst the houses were prorogued in the summer of 1628. However, the removal of the 'grievance of grievances' only allowed other concerns of members to rise to the top of the agenda, namely Charles's continued collection of tonnage and poundage and the promotion of anti-Calvinists in the church (see pp. 68–69). Since these were both aspects of what Charles regarded as the royal prerogative, members of parliament grew fearful of an early dissolution. In an extraordinary scene on 2 March 1629, John Eliot, Denzil Holles and Benjamin Valentine held the speaker in his chair whilst the house passed the Three Resolutions; they stated that anyone who collected or paid tonnage and poundage or who brought in 'innovation in religion' was declared a 'capital enemy to this kingdom and commonwealth'.[10] Shortly afterwards Charles dissolved parliament and arrested nine members of the Commons who had been involved in the events of 2 March.

After 11 years of ruling without parliaments, the king was eventually obliged by the Scottish Prayer Book rebellion of 1637 to call his fourth parliament in 1640; it was known as the Short Parliament because it lasted for only three weeks. Although the king let it be known that 'my necessities are so urgent that there can be no delay [in the granting of supply]', the Commons – as in 1614, 1626 and 1628 – demanded that their grievances be redressed before they made a grant of supply.[11] In particular, members of parliament complained about the fiscal and religious innovations of the Personal Rule (the 11 years from 1629 during which Charles did not call a parliament) and, although Charles did offer to cancel Ship Money[12] in exchange for the immediate grant of 12 subsidies, the parliament collapsed in an atmosphere of mutual distrust. It was typical of Charles that he attributed the failure of the Short Parliament to 'some few cunning and ill-affectioned men'.[13]

1625–40: a 'crisis of parliaments'?

Despite the 11-year gap that occurred between the meeting of Charles's third and fourth parliaments, it makes sense to treat the Short Parliament as a continuation of the parliaments of the 1620s. In particular, in 1640, as in 1625, the king still possessed the ability to call, prorogue and dissolve parliaments at will. This was to change within two months of the meeting of the Long Parliament in November 1640.

Clearly the crown–parliament relationship was a difficult one during this period. However, the Whig view that this was merely an aspect of an ongoing, ideologically inspired constitutional struggle between the early Stuarts and their subjects is now no longer generally held. Charles and Buckingham were not set upon erecting despotic rule, nor was parliament determined to usurp the monarchical prerogative. Revisionist historians have contended instead that political tensions sprang from what they have called a 'functional breakdown' – the impossibility of members of parliament serving the demands of their king and their localities simultaneously during time of war. However, not all historians have accepted this view, arguing that war alone is insufficient as an explanation for the level of conflict. They contend that difficulties in parliaments were in part a consequence of the pressures of war and in part a consequence of broader political considerations induced by the growing distrust of Charles and the advance of the anti-Calvinists (see pp. 68–69).

The Long Parliament

The parliament that first sat in November 1640 is known as the Long Parliament because it sat continuously until April 1653; though after December 1648 it is variously referred to as the Rump, or Purged Parliament, since it had been purged by the army. It sat again briefly on two separate occasions in 1659–60.

1640–42

During the first 18 months of the Long Parliament Charles was obliged to surrender fundamental aspects of the royal prerogative. He gave his assent to acts that obliged him to call parliaments at least once every 3 years for at least 50 days and stated that he could no longer dissolve parliament without its assent – the Triennial Act and Act Against Forcible Dissolution respectively. He was also compelled to agree to the abolition of prerogative devices, fiscal and administrative, which had sustained his rule without parliaments for 11 years. However, from the summer of 1641 parliament proceeded to demand the right to nominate the king's advisers and even to control the army. From 1642 onwards elements in both the Lords and the Commons exercised the king's executive powers on his behalf, and issued ordinances which they claimed had the force of statute even though they had not received the royal assent. How had this come about?

In the first instance, having suffered defeat in the second Bishops' War and thereafter being obliged to pay the Scots £850 a day until a permanent settlement was devised which was also acceptable to parliament, Charles was compelled to allow parliament to continue to sit. This provided his opponents with a platform from which they attacked the hated personnel and machinery of the Personal Rule – notably Laud and Strafford, Ship Money, the Courts of Star Chamber and High Commission, forest fines and knighthood fines.

Even though by September 1641 the king had assented to all of parliament's demands, the reforming zeal of some members of parliament nevertheless remained. To a significant extent this was because the royal concessions had been accompanied with a palpable bad grace, raising a concern as to how far Charles could be trusted not to try to regain what he had conceded. Indeed, this fear was crystallised in May 1641 when Pym revealed that Charles was implicated in a plot to release Strafford from the Tower and to raise troops to threaten parliament with a dissolution (the first Army Plot). In order to secure the concessions already obtained, Pym and his Junto (close advisers and supporters) therefore sought not simply to restrain the royal prerogative but to abrogate to parliament key aspects of it, such as the right to nominate royal ministers. Following the Irish rebellion of October 1641 – since it was out of the question that Charles could be trusted to lead the army which all agreed must be raised – Pym demanded that parliament take control of any such force. For some members of parliament, already disaffected by the use of attainder to remove

Strafford, this was too radical a suggestion and they therefore lent their support to the king, encouraged to do so also because of the stance he had taken on religious issues (see pp. 68–69). When Pym sought a vote on the Grand Remonstrance, a document which listed the 'multiplied evils and corruption' since 1625 and sought constitutional innovations to redress these grievances, it passed the Commons by only 11 votes.

The Civil War that broke out in 1642 was thus not the inevitable consequence of a 'rising' Commons bent upon restraining the crown prerogative from 1603 or even earlier. This is proved in two main ways. Firstly, the political fault lines in 1642 were vertical, not horizontal. In other words, the opposing elements in 1642 were bicameral in nature. Secondly, the key factors necessary for a civil war – roughly equally balanced sides, the absence of a settlement between those sides, and an ideological issue over which to fight (control of the army) – only became simultaneously present in the system as late as the end of 1641. There had been no 'high road' to the English Civil War.

1642–49

There are three particularly noticeable features about parliament during this period. Firstly, its composition was radically altered. With the bishops having been excluded from the Lords in early 1642, and with many lay peers absenting themselves, the upper chamber was reduced to a potential nucleus of around 30 by the end of 1642. Average attendance fell from 59 in January 1642 to only 15 in December. Similarly, the Commons was reduced to an active membership of below 200, though between 1645 and 1648 'recruiter' elections returned about 275 new members. Secondly, it fashioned an executive machinery which ultimately proved highly successful in mobilising resources for the war effort. Ordinances passed by the two houses had the force of statutes and a series of committees of both houses possessed extensive powers. Meanwhile, in their claim to control the judicial system the houses ordered a new Great Seal to be made, prompting Hyde to remark that the houses now seemed determined to assume 'sovereign jurisdiction in civil matters'.[14] Thirdly, there emerged in parliament rival bicameral groupings labelled by contemporaries as Presbyterians and Independents. These groupings were highly fluid and do not amount to political parties though they did possess opposing ideologies; the former agitating for a negotiated settlement with the king and the establishment of a national Presbyterian church, whilst the latter sought to win the war decisively and impose a religious settlement which permitted liberty to tender consciences.

Arguing that the parliamentary trinity was indivisible, the king called a 'royalist' parliament to Oxford in 1644; about 40 peers and over 100 members of the Commons attended. This assembly argued that the Junto had 'speciously pretended the defence of the rights and privileges of Parliament' while in fact 'cancelling all the liberties and privileges of Parliament'.[15] The experiment was not a success for the king, especially because this parliament sought a negotiated settlement with the houses at Westminster whereas Charles intended to reimpose his authority through military victory.

The Great Seal of the Commonwealth of England, 1651, depicting the members of the Rump Parliament, which exercised sovereign powers between 1649 and 1653.

The composition of the Long Parliament, already significantly changed during the period 1641–42, was radically altered for a second time on 6 December 1648. During the course of 1647 the army had become radicalised, protesting that it was 'no mere mercenary army' and apparently imbued with Leveller ideals such as that there should be regular elections.[16] In the aftermath of the second Civil War, Charles having been declared to be 'the capital and grand author of our troubles [who should be brought] to justice for the treason, blood and mischief he is . . . guilty of', the interests and ambitions of the army were placed in jeopardy when parliament reopened negotiations with Charles. Thus, in order to prevent a betrayal of all that they had fought for, the army purged the Commons of those they believed opposed bringing the king to trial. On 6 December 1648 Colonel Pride arrested 45 members of the Commons and excluded a further 186. A total of 86 others withdrew in protest. Seeing which way the wind was blowing, the House of Lords had already effectively ceased to sit.

On 4 January the purged Commons (usually referred to as the Rump) passed an astonishing resolution in which they protested:

that the Commons . . . , being chosen by and representing the people, have the supreme power in this nation; and . . . that whatsoever is enacted and declared for law by the Commons in parliament assembled has the force of law . . . although the consent and concurrence of the King and House of Lords be not had thereunto.[17]

In March 1649, following the execution of the king in January, the Rump passed acts formally abolishing the monarchy and House of Lords. Henceforth, England was to be governed by the Commons alone, as depicted on the new Great Seal of the Commonwealth. This development would have been inconceivable without the events of the Civil Wars and the radicalisation of the army.

The extraordinary mistrust which had built up between Charles and a powerful section of his subjects thus created circumstances which led to the destruction of the parliamentary trinity and the mutilation of the traditional body politic. The regicide itself was not perpetrated by the political nation as represented in the Commons, but instead was the inevitable consequence of a military coup.

The parliaments of the Interregnum, 1649–60

In 1649, for the only time in its history, England began an experiment with republican forms of government that was to last for 11 years. The discussion of the crown–parliament relationship which has featured thus far in this book is therefore temporarily suspended and replaced by an examination of the various constitutional experiments of the 1650s, culminating in the Restoration of the monarchy in 1660. In this respect this is an important period because the nature of the Restoration is largely defined by the experiments in government which preceded it.

The Rump and the Nominated Assembly, 1648–53

Until December 1653 first the Rump (December 1648–April 1653) and then the Nominated Assembly (July 1653–December 1653) assumed supreme legislative power.

The Rump was ideologically flawed, and it is perhaps not surprising that it was short lived. Only a minority of its members were positively committed to a belief in the Commonwealth, others having supported the Rump as merely a necessary means to kill the king. Indeed, in 1650 a majority of members of the Council of State – the new executive machinery – refused to take the Engagement, an oath in which they approved of the regicide. Divisions of opinion combined with threats to its authority – from the Levellers, Ireland, the royalists and the Dutch – resulted in a steady decline in the Rump's legislative record, from 125 acts in 1649 to only 44 in 1652. Having done little to further the godly reforms advocated by the army – and apparently about to sanction fresh elections which would probably have resulted in the return of members of parliament antagonistic to the soldiers' wishes – Cromwell concluded that the Rump 'would never answer those ends which God, His people, and the whole nation expected from them'.[18] On 20 April 1653 Cromwell, accompanied by musketeers, therefore entered parliament and dissolved it by force.

The Rump's successor, the Nominated Assembly, was inspired by the fifth monarchist Thomas Harrison.[19] It was composed of 139 'persons fearing God, and of approved fidelity and honesty', all of whom had not been elected but selected by army officers. Cromwell expected the assembly 'to usher in things that God has promised, which have been prophesied of'.[20] Although the assembly passed 29 acts, the four-fifths of its members who were gentry became increasingly fearful of the intentions of the radical minority, especially their determination to abolish tithes. Thus, in order to deny the radicals a platform, the moderate majority surrendered their power back to Cromwell on 12 December 1653.

Each of the constitutional experiments of this period failed largely because pressure from the army induced reactionary processes which in turn threatened the army's programme.

The Protectorate, 1653–59

The army now set about implementing England's first written Constitution, devised by Major-General John Lambert. The principal feature of the Instrument of Government was its stipulation that government henceforth was to be by 'a single person and a Parliament'. The 'single person' was to take the title of lord protector, a position to which Cromwell was appointed for life. He was to rule with a Council of State and with parliaments that would be elected triennially and sit for a minimum of five months. After a total of nearly 13 years of continuous sitting, parliaments once again became much more infrequent.

However, they did not become any more harmonious than hitherto. For the large part this was an inevitable consequence of Cromwell's attempting to use parliaments as a means to further a godly reformation, especially his ambition to provide a greater 'liberty to tender consciences'. Unfortunately, religious toleration was associated with political dissent, particularly since the emergence of the radical Protestant sects such as the Quakers. Thus it was necessary for Cromwell to maintain the army as a bulwark against the forces of religious intolerance. However, since this in turn necessitated the continuing levy of the hated assessment tax, the electorate and their representatives became increasingly disaffected to the regime. Only if Cromwell had sacrificed either his commitment to the provision of 'liberty to tender consciences' or his desire to work with freely elected assemblies might he have achieved stable republican government.

When the First Protectorate Parliament launched an assault upon the principle of liberty to tender consciences, Cromwell dissolved the assembly at the earliest possible constitutional opportunity, on 22 January 1655. However, having inaugurated a war against Spain, he was obliged to meet with the Second Protectorate Parliament in September 1656. Once again members initiated an attack upon what they regarded as religious blasphemies, especially Quakerism. Indeed, their vicious treatment of the Quaker James Nayler persuaded Cromwell that the single-chamber parliament required some sort of check, otherwise members' religious intolerance might well threaten even Baptists and Independents.

This was the background to the replacement of the Instrument of Government with the Humble Petition and Advice, a second written constitution produced by an element of the political nation eager to diminish the influence of the army. Famously it offered Cromwell the kingship, an offer he eventually declined in May 1657 – partly because he did not want to antagonise the army, but more especially because he did not want to be indebted to the civilian authors of the Humble Petition and because he firmly believed that God had 'blasted the very title [of king]'.[21] Otherwise, Cromwell accepted the new constitution which, in a number of respects, did not seem new at all. Notably, since Cromwell was now permitted to nominate an 'Other House' of between 40 and 70 people, parliament once again became bicameral in form. Moreover, designed to prevent a recurrence of the sort of purges which the council (acting within the terms of the Instrument) had perpetrated upon the First and Second Protectorate Parliaments, henceforth members could only be excluded 'by judgement and consent' of parliament.[22] Several other clauses marked a revival of the privileges enjoyed by early Stuart parliaments. The resort to the familiar was also evident in Cromwell's second installation as lord protector; in the ceremony on 26 June 1657 he wore a robe of purple velvet lined with ermine and carried a gold sceptre. To many observers he must have appeared a king in all but name.

After Cromwell's death in September 1658 his nominated successor, his eldest son Richard, assumed the position of lord protector. However, the reactionary processes which had preceded his accession came to a temporary halt in 1659. Assailed on one side by an army suspicious of his intentions and on the other by a vociferous republican contingent previously excluded by the Instrument but now back in parliament, Richard fell from power in April 1659. The subsequent 12 months saw the Rump Parliament return twice and eventually – under the auspices of George Monck, commander-in-chief of the armed forces in Scotland – the readmission of those members excluded by Pride's Purge in December 1648. The reconvened Long Parliament finally dissolved itself on 16 March 1660, having already set in place procedures for the meeting of a freely elected parliament – the first such since November 1640. This parliament – the so-called Convention Parliament – declared on 8 May 1660 that 'it can no way be doubted but that His Majesty's [i.e. Charles II's] right and title to his crowns and kingdoms was [in] every way completed by the death of his most royal father, without the ceremony or solemnity of a proclamation'.[23] In other words, the Convention was in effect declaring that the Interregnum had officially never existed. Thus, from 1660 the parliamentary trinity of crown, Lords and Commons again became the established form of government.

1648–60: a meaningless experiment?

As noted above, the conservative reaction to the revolutionary events of 1648–49 gathered strength in face of the collapse of stable government in 1659 and thus created the circumstances for the Restoration, an event by no means inevitable even as late as 1659. Moreover, the nature of the Restoration settlement was defined by the events of the 1650s: only the trinity of crown, Lords and Commons seemed able to provide stable government. As such, the collective memory of this period played an important role in the parliaments of Restoration England and imbued the crown with an irreducible core of support.

Religion and the collapse of the national church, 1625–60

The first half of this period is dominated by the advance of anti-Calvinists in the church and the prosecution of Laudian reforms. This process reached its apogee with the publication of a set of Canons in 1640 but was then halted and ultimately reversed during the first two years of the Long Parliament. Dislocation caused by the Civil Wars, the abolition of an episcopalian church hierarchy and the killing of the king encouraged the fragmentation of Protestant unity, so that by the 1650s there had emerged a variety of radical Protestant sects who regarded only God, not the crown, as the head of their church.

The advance of the anti-Calvinists, 1625–40

Since Elizabeth I had formed the famous religious *via media*, the theology of the Church of England had always been Calvinist, the main tenet of which was predestination – the belief that a minority of sinful men were predestined to salvation by the intervening grace of God. A number of men who questioned this belief – Buckeridge, Howson, Neile, Cosin and Laud – had already enjoyed preferment before 1625, probably as a consequence of the influence of Buckingham and Charles over James. Nevertheless, unlike his son, James never became indelibly associated with only one faction and successfully maintained a broad range of opinion in the national church.

Shortly after Charles came to the throne, the direction of the English church shifted distinctly away from Calvinism. By the summer of 1628 all the English sees apart from Lincoln, Salisbury, Worcester and Canterbury were occupied by allies of Laud. Particularly distressing to members of parliament was the fact that Richard Montagu, the author of *A new gag for an old goose* (1624) and *Appello Caesarem* (1625) – tracts in which he denied that the Church of England was essentially Calvinist and made favourable comparisons with the Church of Rome – was now nominated as bishop of Chichester. Two other royalist divines, Robert Sibthorpe and Roger Manwaring, had further enflamed religious sensitivities by preaching sermons in which they supported Charles's collection of the Forced Loan in 1627.

All of this encouraged members of parliament to challenge the king's use of his prerogative as supreme governor of the church, though they recognised that in this respect there were severe limits to their influence. Thus, a committee on religion in February 1629 resolved upon petitioning the king so that he 'would be graciously pleased to confer bishoprics, and other ecclesiastical preferments, with the advice of his Privy Council, upon learned, pious and orthodox men'.[24]

More ominous was their assertion of the Calvinist credentials of the Church of England.

This process of polarisation continued during the Personal Rule, especially after Neile and Laud were appointed to the sees of York and Canterbury in 1632 and 1633 respectively. The situation became yet more volatile when serious political grievances were added to the Calvinists' resentment of the Laudian religious programme of the 1630s. In particular, there was disquiet at the advancement of churchmen in what had for long been secular institutions. For instance, when Bishop Juxon was appointed lord treasurer in 1636 he became the first cleric to hold that post since the fifteenth century. An enhanced clerical influence was responsible for the use of secular courts for religious ends, notably Star Chamber. These were circumstances which many associated with the pre-Reformation church and in turn they led to a general belief in the existence of a popish plot. Indeed, this notion was fuelled when Convocation continued to sit, unprecedentedly, beyond the dissolution of the Short Parliament and produced a set of Canons including the famous Etc. Oath, demanding that the clergy would never consent 'to alter the government of this Church by archbishops, bishops, deans and archdeacons etc . . .'. Another Canon took to a new extreme the doctrine of divine right and anticipated the famous non-resistance oath of 1661. It stipulated that:

> kings should rule and command in their several dominions all persons of what rank or estate soever, whether ecclesiastical or civil, and that they should restrain and punish with the temporal sword all stubborn and wicked doers . . . For subjects to bear arms against their kings, offensive or defensive, upon any pretence whatsoever, is at least to resist the powers which are ordained of God; and though they do not invade but only resist, St Paul tells them plainly they shall receive to themselves damnation.[25]

A negative reformation, 1640–46

The Long Parliament provided the Calvinists with a platform from which they set about redressing their grievances, emasculating the jurisdiction of the prerogative courts of Star Chamber and High Commission and then proceeding to attack the institution of episcopacy – perhaps the most serious assault on crown authority that this period had yet witnessed.

With the support of the Presbyterian Scots, petitions to parliament were drawn up requesting the root and branch abolition of episcopacy as 'a main cause and occasion of many foul evils, pressures and grievances'.[26] Though the king made it plain in a speech in January 1641 that he could not contemplate 'the taking away of their [i.e. the bishops'] voice in parliament . . . [since this was] . . . one of the fundamental institutions of the kingdom', he was nevertheless forced to give his assent in February 1642 to the Bishops' Exclusion Act, forbidding the bishops from sitting in the Lords.[27] However, the ability to nominate bishops was a key aspect of the royal prerogative and, since they were effective agents of the crown, one which Charles was not prepared to relinquish. In fact, as the ambition to abolish episcopacy came increasingly to be associated with a breakdown in law

and order – especially after parliament passed a series of resolutions on
1 September 1641 outlawing the Laudian innovations – many members of the
political nation began to transfer their support to the king.

Thereafter, parliament continued its attack upon the established church in a
piecemeal fashion. In August 1643 ordinances sought to cleanse the churches of
what were thought to be popish symbols; all crucifixes, crosses, images and
pictures relating to the Virgin Mary and persons of the Trinity were to be
destroyed; and candles, tapers and basins were to be removed from communion
tables. Under pressure from the Scots, the Prayer Book was formally outlawed
only in January 1645 and was replaced by a new service book, the Directory of
Public Worship. Finally, the title and authority of bishops was abolished in
October 1646. Nevertheless, it is notable that nothing was done expressly to
challenge the basis of the Elizabethan acts of supremacy and uniformity. Charles
was still head of the national church, even if it was not entirely clear what the
nature of that national church was.

Defining a new national church, 1646–54

Most members of parliament were committed to the replacement of the Anglican
church by a new form of national church, though there was severe disagreement
about what form this new church should take. In 1645 the Westminster Assembly
– the parliamentary committee on religion – devised a form of Presbyterian
church intended to appease the Scots, military allies of parliament since 1643.
However, this was so different from the Presbyterian system north of the border
that the Scots dismissed it as a 'lame Erastian presbytery'. Moreover, there was a
sizeable minority in England, represented especially by the soldiers, who
resented the prospect of having to worship in any national church. This element,
known as the Independents, saw that their religious interests would be served by
opting out of a national church. By 1654 this situation had led to such a
proliferation of religious sects, some of which threatened the stability of secular
affairs, that Cromwell attempted to improve ecclesiastical discipline with his
bodies of Triers and Ejectors. The Triers were a national body set up to examine
all new clergy before allowing them to preach, and the Ejectors were commissioners appointed in each county to expel 'scandalous, ignorant and insufficient
ministers and schoolmasters'.

The failure of the Cromwellian church, 1654–59

Each of the written constitutions of the Protectorate contained important clauses
relating to religion. In language which was echoed by the Humble Petition and
Advice, the Instrument of Government insisted that Protestants even 'though
differing in judgement from the doctrine, worship or discipline publicly held forth
[i.e. the Presbyterian church settlement] shall be protected in . . . [the] exercise of
their religion' so long as they do not 'practice licentiousness'.[28]

Yet it was one thing to espouse toleration in a written constitution and quite
another to put it into practice. Indeed, Cromwell's ambition for a 'godly
reformation' and the severe measures with which this came to be associated

during the rule of the major-generals between 1655 and 1657 induced a conservative reaction. In order to appease these reactionary forces in the Protectorate parliaments, Cromwell was forced to sacrifice some of the more radical Protestant sects such as the Socinians and the Quakers. It was not an atmosphere in which a long-lasting religious settlement was ever likely to be established. Above all, it shaped the nature of the Restoration settlement because settled government seemed to walk hand in hand with divinely ordained monarchy only.

Document case study

The language of misunderstanding?

4.1 John Pym's reply to Strafford's last speech in his defence, 13 April 1641

It is the law that doth entitle a king to the allegiance and service of his people; it entitles the people to the protection and justice of the King . . . The law is the boundary, the measure between the King's prerogative and the people's liberty. Whilst these move in their own orbs they are a support and a security to one another; the prerogative a cover and defence to the liberty of the people, and the people by their liberty are entitled to be a foundation to the prerogative; but if these bounds be so removed that they enter into contestation and conflict one of these mischiefs must ensue: if the prerogative of the King overwhelm the liberty of the people it will be turned into tyranny; if liberty undermine the prerogative, it will grow into anarchy.

Source: John Rushworth (ed.), *Historical collections of private passages of state*, 8 vols., London, 1659–1701, vol. 2, pp. 661–63, reprinted in J. P. Kenyon (ed.), *The Stuart Constitution: documents and commentary*, 2nd edition, Cambridge, 1986, p. 196.

4.2 The Grand Remonstrance of November 1641

The Commons in this parliament assembled, having . . . for the space of twelve months wrestled with great dangers and fears . . . [which have] . . . extinguished the liberty, peace and prosperity of this kingdom . . . and exceedingly weakened and undermined the foundation and strength of [His Majesty's] own royal throne, do yet find an abounding malignity and opposition in those parties and factions who have been the cause of those evils . . . and [who] foment jealousies between the King and Parliament.

Source: Rushworth (ed.), *Historical collections*, vol. 4, pp. 437–51, reprinted in Kenyon (ed.), *Stuart Constitution*, p. 209.

4.3 *His Majesty's answer to a printed book*, 26 May 1642

[Those responsible for all our troubles are] a faction of Malignant, Schismatical and Ambitious persons, whose design is, and always has been, to alter the frame of the Government both of Church and State, and to subject both King and People to their own lawless arbitrary power and Government.

Source: Christopher W. Daniels and John Morrill, *Charles I*, Cambridge, 1988, p. 100.

4.4 *A declaration of the Lords and Commons in parliament concerning His Majesty's proclamation of the 27 May 1642*, 6 June 1642

The High Court of Parliament is not only a court of judicature, enabled by the laws to adjudge and determine the rights and liberties of the kingdom, against such patents and grants of his Majesty as are prejudicial thereunto, although strengthened both by his personal command and by his proclamation under the Great Seal; but it is likewise a council, to provide for the necessities, prevent the imminent dangers, and preserve the public peace and safety of the kingdom, and to declare the King's pleasure in those things as are requisite thereunto; and what they do herein hath the stamp of royal authority, although his Majesty, seduced by evil counsel, do in his own person oppose or interrupt the same; for the King's supreme and royal pleasure is exercised and declared in this high court of law and counsel after a more eminent and obligatory manner than it can be by personal act or resolution of his own.

Source: *Lords' journals*, vol. 5, p. 341, reprinted in Kenyon (ed.), *Stuart Constitution*, p. 227.

4.5 The king's *Answer to the nineteen propositions*, 18 June 1642

Therefore the [judicatory] power, legally placed in both houses, is more than sufficient to restrain the power of tyranny, and without the power which is now asked from us we shall not be able to discharge that trust which is the end of monarchy, since this would be a total subversion of the fundamental laws, and that excellent constitution of this kingdom . . . since to the power of punishing (which is already in your hands according to law)[a] if the power of preferring[b] be added, we shall have nothing left for us to look on, since the encroaching of one of these estates upon the power of the other is unhappy in the effects . . . since this power of at most a joint government in us with our councillors (or rather, our guardians) will return us to the worst kind of minority, and make us despicable both at home and abroad and beget eternal factions and dissensions.

[a] A reference to the Commons' ability to inaugurate impeachment proceedings.
[b] A reference to the Commons' determination to nominate the king's councillors.

Source: Rushworth (ed.), *Historical collections*, vol. 5, pp. 728, 730–32, reprinted in Kenyon (ed.), *Stuart Constitution*, p. 19.

Document case-study questions

1 Using the knowledge that you have gained from Chapter 1, how far do you agree about the powers of the High Court of Parliament as outlined in 4.4?

2 What explanation do 4.2 and 4.4 put forward for the emergence of jealousies 'between the King and Parliament'? How far does this explanation agree with that offered by the king in 4.3?

3 Read 4.1 and 4.5. How similar are Pym's and Charles's opinions about the law? In the light of your answer, assess the effectiveness of Charles's *Answer to the nineteen propositions*.

Notes and references

We should like to thank Stephen Walmsley and Greg Paul of The Manchester Grammar School for their comments on this chapter.

1 L. J. Reeve, *Charles I and the road to personal rule*, Cambridge, 1989, p. 4.

2 Conrad Russell, *The causes of the English Civil War*, Oxford, 1990, p. 207.

3 See J. P. Kenyon (ed.), *The Stuart Constitution: documents and commentary*, 2nd edition, Cambridge, 1986, p. 86.

4 Richard Cust, *The Forced Loan and English politics, 1626–1628*, Oxford, 1987, p. 88.

5 Quoted in R. Sherwood, *The court of Oliver Cromwell*, Cambridge, 1977, pp. 135–36.

6 B. Coward, *Oliver Cromwell*, Harlow, 1991, p. 106.

7 Coward, *Cromwell*, p. 62.

8 Blair Worden, *The Rump Parliament*, Cambridge, 1974, p. 69.

9 Quoted in David L. Smith, *A history of the modern British Isles, 1603–1707: the double crown*, Oxford, 1998, p. 72.

10 For the Three Resolutions see Kenyon (ed.), *Stuart Constitution*, p. 71.

11 Quoted in David L. Smith, *The Stuart parliaments, 1603–1689*, London, 1999, p. 121.

12 It was an established right of the crown to levy money from coastal towns and counties during national emergencies in order to build a fleet. However, not only did Charles levy Ship Money with unprecedented frequency (every year between 1634 and 1639, whereas this tax was normally collected every few decades), but also from 1635 he extended the tax to cover the whole of England and Wales.

13 Quoted in Smith, *Stuart parliaments*, p. 121.

14 Quoted in Smith, *Stuart parliaments*, p. 130.

15 Quoted in Smith, *Stuart parliaments*, p. 131.

16 Quoted in Smith, *Stuart parliaments*, p. 133.

17 Quoted in Smith, *Stuart parliaments*, p. 135.

18 Quoted in Smith, *Stuart parliaments*, p. 137.

19 The fifth monarchists accepted the prophecies in the books of Revelation and Daniel in the Old Testament. These predicted that the four great empires of Babylon, Persia, Greece and Rome would soon be followed by the fifth monarchy in which Christ would rule with his saints for one thousand years, culminating in the day of judgement.

20 Quoted in Smith, *History*, p. 183.

21 See David L. Smith, *Oliver Cromwell: politics and religion in the English Revolution 1640–1658*, Cambridge, 1991, p. 57.

22 The Instrument and Humble Petition can be found in Kenyon (ed.), *Stuart Constitution*, pp. 308–13, 324–30.

23 Smith, *Stuart parliaments*, p. 146.

24 Kenyon (ed.), *Stuart Constitution*, p. 142.

25 For the Canons of 1640 see Kenyon (ed.), *Stuart Constitution*, pp. 149–53.

26 Quoted in Smith, *History*, p. 116.

27 For this speech see Kenyon (ed.), *Stuart Constitution*, pp. 17–18.

28 See note 22.

5
Charles II and James VII and II, 1660–88

The personalities of Charles II and James VII and II

The character of Charles II, 1660–85

At the age of 21, having failed in his attempts to regain the throne after the execution of his father in 1649, Charles was forced into exile from 1651. The following years were spent in France and then, from 1656, the Spanish Netherlands. Perhaps unsurprisingly, he became 'infinitely distrustful'.[1] The marquis of Halifax, a leading privy councillor later in Charles's reign, did 'not believe that ever he trusted any man or any set of men so entirely as not to have some secrets in which they had no share; as this might make him less well served, so in some degree it might make him the less imposed upon'.[2]

Over 1.8 metres [6 feet] tall and possessed of an extraordinary mane of very dark brown, almost black, curly hair, Charles was an impressive, if not classically handsome, figure. 'Odd's fish,' he commented to Lely after the latter had completed the royal portrait, 'I am an ugly fellow.'[3] He had an easy manner and ready charm and was the most accessible of all the Stuart monarchs, though no one could quite work out where they stood with him. 'He had the greatest art of concealing himself of any man alive,' wrote Burnet, 'so that those about him cannot tell when he is ill or well pleased.'[4] Physically active, he became accomplished at bowls, croquet, tennis and riding, and especially dancing and sailing. Charles was also something of a polymath. His interests ranged from art and architecture to theatre and gardening. He enjoyed maths and chemistry and became a patron of the Royal Society, established by royal charter in 1660. It is true that Charles was lazy but he was not incorrigibly so – as became apparent during the Popish Plot, when his attention to the details of government was impressive. Contrary to general opinion, he was a regular attender of privy council meetings, though, as Pepys noted, ministers had to 'administer business to him as doctors do physic – wrap it up in something to make it less unpleasant'.[5]

Although Charles was married to Catherine of Braganza in 1662, he remained a serial womaniser, often manoeuvring between a number of mistresses from all social classes – by whom he sired at least 17 bastards. 'Restless he rolls about from whore to whore/A merry monarch, scandalous and poor.'[6] Some of these royal mistresses – such as Lucy Walter, Barbara Villiers, Nell Gwynn and Louise de Keroualle – are well known. There is, though, no doubt that there were others, 'nocturnal visitors introduced up the Privy Stairs . . . [though] their numbers, like their identities, remain unknown to history'.[7] Yet the royal marriage remained barren, a circumstance which induced the Exclusion Crisis of 1679–81.

At the time of the Restoration, Charles's principal objective henceforth was to avoid circumstances which might result in his 'going on his travels' again. Nevertheless, for much of his reign he deviated from the wishes of the political nation to such an extent, and employed his prerogative in such a fashion, that he created substantial hostility and suspicion – especially in his attempts to provide toleration to the dissenters and Catholics. Why was this? Firstly, his experiences in exile, especially those occasions when he had enjoyed help from Catholics, had resulted in his being naturally indisposed to religious persecution. Secondly, it may have been because he had some sympathy with Catholicism. After all, a clause in the extraordinary secret treaty with France in 1670 stated that Charles, 'being convinced of the truth of the Roman Catholic religion is resolved to declare it, and to reconcile himself with the Church of Rome as soon as his country's affairs permit'.[8] Moreover, he was received into the Catholic church on his deathbed in 1685. Thirdly, it seems that he had probably accepted the economic and political arguments for toleration, that a state would be richer and more stable as a consequence. Fourthly, by forging an alliance with the dissenters by providing them with toleration, he would create an alternative power base and avoid being beholden to the Anglicans. Finally, like Cromwell, he recognised that the security of his regime would be firmly established only when the various elements in the nation had been united.

Yet Charles never allowed his personal conviction to destroy the prospect of peaceable government. To this end pragmatism and flexibility, the key criteria of successful government, were his watchwords. Like his grandfather, James VI and I, Charles possessed qualities – personal and political – which explain why he became such an effective ruler.

The character of James II, 1685–88

'Never [a] king was proclaimed with more applause than James II . . . I doubt not to see a happy reign', noted the earl of Peterborough in 1685.[9] However, before four years had elapsed James fled in the face of an invasion force headed by his son-in-law, William of Orange, inaugurating what Protestant historians have labelled the 'Glorious Revolution'.

An examination of James's early public pronouncements offers no explanation for this course of events. Within hours of the death of his brother, Charles, the new king announced that he would 'endeavour to preserve this government both in Church and State as it is [now] by law established'. He also promised that just as he would 'never depart from the just rights and prerogative of the Crown, so I shall never invade any man's property'.[10] The loyal addresses duly rolled in. It is tempting to accuse James of having been deliberately disingenuous, but this is probably as unfair as he was misguided. It was James's overriding aim, as he later told the French ambassador, 'to establish the Catholic religion in England so that those who profess it could live as Catholics in complete security'.[11]

Yet James had seriously underestimated the obstacles to his ambition. Firstly, as the French ambassador remarked, 'he [i.e. James] flatters himself that the Anglican Church is so little removed from the Catholic that it should not be difficult to bring the majority of them to declare themselves openly. He has told me several times that they are Roman Catholics without knowing it.'[12] Secondly, James fundamentally failed to appreciate that most Englishmen equated Catholicism with arbitrary government and therefore opposed that form of religion with a peculiar intensity. For these reasons James was forced to deploy the royal prerogative in ways which ultimately disaffected the majority of the political nation, because he threatened to destroy Anglicanism and the structures by which it remained materially and jurisdictionally pre-eminent.

James appears to have converted to Catholicism in about 1669, though he did not stop attending Anglican services until 1673 – the year in which he took as his second wife the Catholic Mary Beatrice of Modena. James had probably been impressed by the conversion in 1668 of his military hero, the French commander, Turenne, although it is also likely that the authoritarian nature of the creed appealed to his military nature. Certainly he was an accomplished soldier. During the Interregnum, whilst an exile in France, he first joined the French army and latterly enlisted with the Spanish forces and fought at the Battle of the Dunes in 1659. At the Restoration he was created lord high admiral and fought successfully in the Battle of Sole Bay in 1665 and then again at Southwold Bay in 1672. Having converted to Catholicism, he was forced to resign from office in 1673 according to the terms of the Test Act, though he was granted a special exemption from the second Test Act of 1678 without which he would have been required to surrender his seat in the Lords.

Both before and after his conversion, there is an unpleasant aura of Cromwellian self-righteousness about James, bolstered by his sense that God had repeatedly shown him favour – for example, by allowing him to escape from England successfully in 1648 and by saving him from death in a shipwreck in 1682. But, above all, God had preserved him from being excluded from the succession according to the schemes of Shaftesbury (see pp. 80–81). As a consequence James's public manner was gratingly arrogant, as was quickly demonstrated by his breathless impatience with the parliament of 1685. Unsurprisingly, he was utterly intolerant of any who obstructed the royal will and refused to countenance either compromise or concessions, believing that this had been a fatal flaw in the character of his father. 'Get ye gone,' he told the fellows of Magdalen College, Oxford, after they had refused his nomination for president; 'know I am your King and I command you to be gone.'[13]

James's swaggering self-confidence endowed him with a propensity for monumental tactlessness such as when, in the spring of 1687, he staged a public entry into London for Ferdinand D'Adda, the newly appointed papal nuncio; and when he determined to prosecute seven bishops in 1688 for failing to read the reissued Declaration of Indulgence (see p. 88). Yet such actions are probably also explained by a profound inability to empathise with the sensibilities of others, a consequence of his narrow-mindedness. As the lord chancellor, Clarendon, had

A portrait of James II.

observed at an early date, the king's determination was sustained 'rather from an obstinacy in his will, which he defended by aversion from the debate, than by the constancy of his judgement'.[14]

Having convinced himself that the forces of his son-in-law, William of Orange, were not destined to be sent against England, James was devastated when it became clear that William was intent upon launching an invasion. This realisation induced in James an intense insecurity and persecution complex that had been apparent at the start of the reign and was thereafter signalled by his aggressive self-confidence. In the autumn of 1688 – as elements of the political nation defected to William, including his daughter, Princess Anne – James lost his resolve to go on. He took flight to France in December, only once thereafter attempting to recapture the throne by means of a campaign in Ireland that culminated in his defeat by William at the Battle of the Boyne in 1690. James henceforth returned to exile in France where he spent his time in prayer, creating devotional writings and subjecting his flesh to acts of penance, including wearing an iron chain studded with spikes around his thighs. 'May I always be prepared for death, whenever it pleases You to call me to You,' he prayed.[15] When the end finally came on 5 September 1701, his corpse was cut up and his heart buried at the nunnery of Chaillot.

If the character of Charles II has an affinity with that of James I, that of James II is strikingly similar to Charles I. Both men 'suffered from energy' and were conviction politicians. Like his father, James regarded all forms of opposition as subversive. As such, James considered that it had to be either suppressed or rooted out in the interests of what he firmly believed was the common good.

Parliaments and politics, 1660–88

A study of political events during the years 1660–88 is perhaps best approached by examining the period in two parts, from the Restoration to the end of the Exclusion Crisis in 1681 and from 1681 to James II's flight in 1688. During the first of these periods the crown suffered a number of largely self-inflicted political embarrassments, such as the decision in 1672 to suspend repayment of all previous loans (the so-called 'Stop of the Exchequer') and a miserable performance in the third Dutch War. Nevertheless, parliament was also responsible for confounding the ambition of the crown, particularly in its determination to prevent the king from using his prerogative to suspend all penal laws against both Catholic and Protestant nonconformists. But by far the most significant threat to the authority of the crown occurred in the Exclusion Crisis (1679–81) when the opposition ultimately sought to exclude James, duke of York, from the succession because he was a Catholic. During the second period the crown moved to assert its authority, though historians have been unable to agree how strong the English monarchy actually became in the 1680s and to what extent 'liberty and property' were placed in danger. Indeed, the Whig interpretation that these years witnessed a concerted attempt, by James in particular, to establish an absolutist state along the lines of seventeenth-century European regimes has recently met with criticism, especially from John Miller.[16]

1660–81: parliament ascendant?

In that the main elements of the constitutional settlement of 1660 turned back the clock to 1641, thereby deliberately reaffirming the reforming legislation to which Charles I had given his assent in the early stages of the Long Parliament, it has been customary to stress the weaknesses of the restored monarchy rather than its strengths. Certainly parliament's decision not to revive Star Chamber, the Council of the North Marches and the Court of High Commission ensured that the coercive powers of the crown remained significantly diminished. Moreover, not only did the financial legislation of 1641 remain in place – depriving the crown of many of its feudal revenues and an ability to raise funds by prerogative taxation like Ship Money – but also the Convention Parliament of 1660 abolished purveyance and the Court of Wards, though they did grant Charles revenues estimated at £1.2 million per annum. If this sum fell short of royal needs, which it consistently did, the monarch could raise extra funds only by means explicitly approved by parliament – the main reason why the Cavalier Parliament met every year, apart from one, between 1661 and 1679. Indeed, it is possible that a shortfall was deliberately contrived, for as one member of parliament told Charles, albeit in the altered circumstances of the 1670s, 'I am for keeping the revenue from being too big, for then you'll need Parliaments.'[17]

The Cavalier Parliament therefore provided members of parliament with a platform from which they could articulate their criticisms of royal policies. The nature of this opposition hardened and became more effective as suspicions of Charles and his government grew. Thus, during the years of the Cabal (1667–73) – a loose-knit group of five ministers, some of whom were either Catholic or Catholic sympathisers – there emerged in parliament a Country opposition headed by members such as Sir William Coventry, Sir Thomas Meres, Lord Cavendish, William Lord Russell and William Sacheverell. This was not an organised 'party' in the modern sense, but a group held together by certain common beliefs: a determination to defend the privileges of parliament against the royal prerogative, an attachment to Protestantism, hostility towards Francophile policies and a fear of the advance of 'popery'.

The Country element appears to have enjoyed significant success, especially in their assault upon Charles's scheme to suspend all penal laws against both Catholic and Protestant dissenters in the Declaration of Indulgence of 15 March 1672. This highlighted a grey area of the prerogative as to whether penal statutes could be suspended by royal instruction. On 4 February 1673 the Commons voted by 168 to 116 that 'penal statutes in matters ecclesiastical cannot be suspended but by act of Parliament'.[18] Not only was Charles forced to withdraw the declaration but also, as the price for securing parliamentary supply, he was obliged to give his assent to a new Test Act in 1673. Since all office holders henceforth had to swear the oaths of supremacy and allegiance and repudiate the Catholic doctrine of transubstantiation, it was clear that Charles's ability to appoint advisers of his own choosing was severely curtailed. Members of parliament had successfully diminished a key aspect of the royal prerogative.

The parliamentary opponents of Charles also began to employ the practice of granting supply only on the basis that it would be spent in a particular way, reviving the appropriation clause that had first been used in the parliament of 1624 (see p. 46). This was resorted to by the Commons in the third Dutch War (1672–74) and in 1677, when they voted money to be spent 'for the speedy building [of] 30 ships of war'.[19] In 1678, in order to provide for the disbandment of the army which had been raised for the abortive Flanders campaign of that spring, they voted a grant of money but tied it to a precise date for the demobilisation to occur – 'a clear infringement of the royal prerogative of peace and war', in Kenyon's view.[20] According to Lord Chancellor Finch, these anti-prerogative clauses tacked onto bills of supply threatened to 'alter the whole frame and constitution of Parliaments'.[21]

Clearly a significant change came over the nature of the parliamentary opposition in the 1670s. In part this was because of continued suspicion of Charles's sympathy for Catholicism and, as apparently signified by the regime of

Louis XIV, a widespread acceptance that popery bred arbitrary government. This fear was articulated in December 1677 with the publication of Andrew Marvell's *An account of the growth of popery and arbitrary government*. Marvell alleged that 'for divers years' a 'design' had been 'carried on to change the lawful government of England into an absolute tyranny, and to convert the established Protestant religion into downright Popery'.[22] In part also it was because in the aftermath of the collapse of the Cabal the Country element had gained the support of Buckingham and, more importantly, the ruthless and gifted Shaftesbury. Consequently, as Geoffrey Holmes has noted, 'the anti-ministerial and anti-Popish forces in parliament after April 1675 [= the fourteenth session of the Cavalier Parliament] ceased to be primarily defensive, checking Charles's misdemeanours and getting him back on to the straight and narrow. Aggression replaced defence.'[23]

Though the Country party did not as yet possess a systematic programme 'to fetter the King', as Lord Conway alleged, it nevertheless sought to restrain the powers of the crown.[24] Alongside tacking anti-prerogative clauses to bills of supply, it sponsored abortive bills for *habeas corpus* and judicial independence. It also sought to remove Danby, Charles's leading minister after the demise of the Cabal. Paradoxically – even though Danby pursued an anti-French, pro-Dutch foreign policy and sought significantly to limit religious toleration – the authoritarian methods he employed disaffected members of parliament who accused him of seeking to establish absolutism on behalf of the king. His bribing of members emboldened Shaftesbury to seek a dissolution of the Cavalier Parliament in the expectation that this would destroy Danby's power base. To this end Shaftesbury encouraged what Holmes has called an 'aggressive disrespect for the prerogative', ultimately claiming that parliament *was* dissolved after it had been prorogued for an unprecedented 15 months by February 1677, an assertion which earned Shaftesbury and others 5 months in the Tower.[25] Ultimately, Danby was dismissed in 1679 as a direct result of an impeachment, though he was the only minister to suffer this fate.

But by far the greatest assault upon the prerogative was the attempt to exclude Charles's brother, James, from the throne; if parliament determined the succession it would destroy the notion of a divinely ordained monarchy. Though James had converted to Catholicism as early as 1669 – and had been officially smoked out as a papist when he was forced to resign his command as lord admiral according to the terms of the first Test Act in 1673 – most members of parliament avoided squaring up to the unthinkable by continuing to hope that Charles's marriage would yet produce an heir. However, the revelations of Titus Oates and Israel Tonge, alleging that there was a Catholic plot to assassinate Charles and put James on the throne, meant that members could prevaricate no longer. In order to secure support for his ambition to exclude James from the succession in favour of Monmouth, the Protestant illegitimate son of Charles, Shaftesbury founded the first political party in English history. His 'Whigs' organised petitions and demonstrations, orchestrated campaigns in three successive general elections (1679–81) and produced a mass of propaganda.

Ultimately they failed, partly because of the political skill of Charles and their opponents, the 'Tories', and partly because of a determination amongst the political elite to avoid another civil war.

The fact that the Country and Whig opponents of Charles only rarely succeeded in their objectives should not obscure their longer-term importance; they were a precursor of the two-party system that became such a feature of English politics in the 1690s and beyond.

Despite the incidents related above, it is seriously misleading to describe parliament as enjoying ascendancy over the crown in this period. This was certainly not an ambition of parliament. Even though it is possible to perceive the emergence of 'sides' in the Commons during these years, it was still the case that disputes were usually the result of factions championing a particular cause. Short-lived and non-ideological, this is reminiscent of crown–parliament relations in the earlier part of the seventeenth century.

It is also worth stressing the restrictions which parliament chose *not* to impose upon the crown in 1660 and shortly thereafter. The monarch was henceforth free to choose their advisers and crown control of the militia was explicitly reaffirmed. The two principal constitutional demands of 1641–48 were thus abandoned in 1660. In 1664 parliament repealed the Triennial Act of 1641 and replaced it with an act which obliged the king to meet parliament every three years but provided no machinery for this to occur and stipulated no minimum period for a session. Driven forward by a determination to avoid a recurrence of the horrors of civil war, members thus deliberately restored monarchical authority. Finally, members sought to bolster the authority of the crown by granting Charles an annual sum of £1.2 million, a greater sum than that which had enabled Charles I to rule without parliaments in the 1630s. When economic recession made it clear that this sum would be difficult to collect, parliament supplemented royal income by introducing the Hearth Tax in 1662. The fact that Charles remained short of money was therefore a consequence of his own extravagance and the vicissitudes of the economy rather than of a determination by members to tie him to parliament.

Therefore, the non-religious aspects of the Restoration Settlement did not in themselves induce troubled relations between crown and parliament. However, in that they collectively restored pre-war fears and tensions, they facilitated opposition to the crown once it was feared that Charles, or his advisers, seemed to be perpetrators of a popish plot, and, since popery was associated with arbitrary government, it had to be resisted. In this sense, as Jonathan Scott has argued, the attempt to exclude James from the succession was a symptom rather than a cause of the crisis; the events of 1679–81 were the real 'Restoration Crisis'.[26]

It is also worth stressing that the Commons' power to coerce the king was limited. They were frustrated in their attempts to put financial pressure on the king after his ordinary revenues (from customs) swelled when the economy improved or when he obtained some money from Louis XIV, or both. Moreover, in any constitutional crisis with the Commons Charles could usually rely upon support from the Lords. Above all, many members of parliament regarded coercion of the monarch as unconstitutional. As Miller points out, '[Charles's] difficulties with Parliament [therefore] owed more to his political insensitivity and poor management than to any new power or assertiveness on the part of the Commons.'[27]

By far the greatest threat to the crown's authority after 1660 was posed, as John Morrill has noted, 'not by the gentry in Parliament, but by the gentry in the provinces'.[28] The abolition of the conciliar courts in 1660 meant that the government was more than ever dependent upon the active consent of the gentry. It is a testament to the consensus politics of the period that the crown usually received their support.

1681–88: towards 'arbitrary government'?

Angus McInnes has suggested that 'by the 1680s England was . . . fast approaching the condition of an absolutist monarchy, a country different only in detail from the classic absolutist states of continental Europe'.[29] Although this opinion has been attacked by John Miller, it is clear that the policies of Charles, from 1681 to 1685, and especially of James, from 1685 to 1688, threatened 'liberties' and the rights of property.

Parliamentary government and free elections were placed in jeopardy. In 1684, benefiting from an improved financial situation, Charles violated the terms of the Triennial Act by failing to call another parliament after a three-year interval. In three-and-a-half years James met with only one parliament for two brief sessions in 1685. When it became clear that this parliament would not repeal the penal laws against Catholics, he began preparations to pack a future parliament and in the meantime issued a Declaration of Indulgence (1687) in which he employed the royal prerogative to suspend the test and corporation acts and penal laws (see pp. 87–88).

Both kings purged government of their opponents, James more extensively than his brother. During the summer of 1681 many Whigs were removed from the commissions of the peace and the lieutenancies. Between 1681 and 1685 a total of 51 new borough charters was issued, providing the king with the right to remove any corporation member of whom he disapproved. (It is worth noting that these revised charters were usually the result of local initiatives rather than royal ones.) By the spring of 1688 James had effected an unprecedented purge of local government: 14 of the 24 lords lieutenant, three-quarters of all justices of the peace and over 1,200 members of town corporations had been dismissed. The Commission for Ecclesiastical Causes was established in 1686 and proceeded to suspend Compton, a bishop who had refused to enforce a declaration outlawing preaching which attacked Catholics. This seemed to presage an assault upon the whole Anglican hierarchy. Moreover, since the commission was reminiscent of the Court of High Commission, abolished in 1641, it was widely held to be illegal.

Judicial independence was increasingly compromised. From as early as 1676 Charles had appointed judges *durante bene placito* ('during the king's pleasure') rather than *quamdiu se bene gesserint* ('for as long as they shall do good'). In the 9 years before his death Charles removed 11 judges. Prior to the Godden versus

Hales Case in June 1686 James dismissed six judges, whom he considered unreliable, in order to ensure that the verdict would uphold his dispensing power.

Property rights and liberty of the press also suffered. In October 1687 the Commission for Ecclesiastical Causes deprived all 25 fellows of Magdalen College, Oxford, of their fellowships for failing to accept either of two Catholic royal nominees as their president. This caused a wave of shock and anger because fellowships were regarded as legal freeholds and the deprivation of the Magdalen fellows therefore represented an attack upon property rights. Sir Roger L'Estrange, who had issued many pamphlets which were important in encouraging the Tory reaction to the Exclusion Crisis, 'conducted in James's reign intensive literary propaganda . . . on behalf of the royal policy'.[30] Finally, using the rebellion of 1685 led by Monmouth (Charles II's illegitimate son) as a justification, James increased the size of his army to 19,778 by the end of 1685.

Despite these developments, it is difficult to agree with McInnes. In Charles's case, he lacked the fixity of purpose required to erect an absolutist regime. Paradoxically, given the nature of the Restoration Settlement and the determination to avoid another civil war, if Charles had intended to enhance his prerogative then the most likely way for this to have occurred was for him to have collaborated with members of parliament rather than to have antagonised them. The final years of his reign are perhaps best seen as the moment in which he at last embraced the principles of his natural supporters, the Tory–Anglicans. It is equally difficult to perceive James as having been intent upon absolutism for its own sake. Rather, he sought to create circumstances in which a parliament would repeal the penal laws against Catholics and dissenters together with the test and corporation acts. In any case, because for much of his reign he expected to be succeeded by the Protestants William and Mary (it was only in June 1688 that James's wife, Mary of Modena, gave birth to a son), why should he have sought to have established an absolutist state for their benefit?

Religion and the Restoration church, 1660–88

Whereas the secular aspects of the Restoration Settlement were surprisingly generous to a wide spectrum of interests, the nature of the Restoration church was narrow and intolerant. Consequently there emerged after 1660 two fairly distinct groups: on the one hand, those who supported the Restoration church, the Anglicans; and on the other hand, those whose consciences would not allow them to worship in the newly defined national church, the dissenters (sometimes called nonconformists). Historians have disagreed over how great was the number of dissenters, but a survey by Bishop Henry Compton of London in 1676 counted nearly 100,000 in an adult population of 2.25 million in England and Wales. It seems likely that the total number was at least two or three times greater than Compton's figure. The extent of nonconformity put the church on the defensive and imbued it with a reluctance to grant any concessions.

The religious differences between these two groups were stiffened by the political grievances and jealousies of the Anglicans; believing that the king's old enemies had benefited sufficiently in the secular sphere, they were determined to prevent their advance in the church. What complicates the history of this period is that Charles did not fall in with the Anglicans, even though as supporters of the royal supremacy and an episcopalian hierarchy they were the monarch's natural allies. Instead, for much of the 1660s and 1670s, for reasons presented on pp. 84–86, Charles seemed a better friend of the dissenters.

Thus, the crown appeared as an enemy of the church. The methods it employed in its quest to allow dissenters to worship *within* the established church – or at least tolerate them outside it – induced a dangerous antagonism between the crown and the Anglicans. Since the latter were most powerfully represented in parliament, this in turn generated political tension between crown and parliament, the Anglicans championing parliament as a check on the crown.

Religion under Charles II

As early as the summer of 1662 the Convention Parliament and its successor, the Cavalier Parliament, had established an exclusive and intolerant church settlement along Anglican lines. Given the disorder which had accompanied the collapse of the Interregnum, it is hardly surprising that Charles II faced parliaments that were reactionary in nature. Sir John Vaughan believed that comprehension would 'subvert the present government'.[31] There was also a palpable relief at being 'freed from the chains of darkness and confusion which the presbyterians and fanatics had brought upon them'.[32] Moreover, the general belief that religious dissent and political subversion walked hand in hand was stiffened as a result of an abortive fifth monarchist rising in London in January 1661 led by Thomas Venner.

All hopes, as Charles had stated in the Declaration of Breda (1660), to 'declare a liberty to tender consciences [so] that no man shall be disquieted or called in question for differences of opinion in matter of religion which do not disturb the peace of the kingdom' therefore quickly evaporated.[33] Two pieces of legislation in particular, neither of which Charles could have vetoed without causing a political crisis, thwarted the royal will. Firstly, in December 1661 the Corporation Act excluded from borough corporations those who would not take the Anglican sacrament. Secondly, in May 1662 the new Act of Uniformity required all ministers to declare their 'unfeigned assent and consent' to everything contained in the new Prayer Book (devised by Convocation over the course of 1661–62) and to use it in their services.[34] Since the new Prayer Book proved objectionable to most dissenters, this act led directly to 936 ministers being deprived of their livings – adding to the total of almost 700 that had already been ejected since 1660. Thus, by the end of 1662 about 18 per cent of ministers in England had been removed from their livings since 1660. Meanwhile, in an attempt to by-pass the intolerance of members of parliament, in October 1660 Charles had sponsored talks between Presbyterians and Anglican clergy at Worcester House. In the consequent Worcester House Declaration of 25 October Charles seemingly made a number of concessions to the Presbyterians, including a promise to restrain bishops' powers by allowing presbyters to be involved with episcopalian jurisdiction. However, after the election of the Cavalier Parliament there was no chance that these concessions would be translated into legislative form. Royal attempts in 1662 to dispense from the provisions of the Act of Uniformity all those who were not ministers of the church were also blocked by parliament, Gilbert Sheldon – then bishop of London – accusing Charles of taking 'liberty to throw down the laws of the land at your pleasure'.[35] All in all, by the end of 1662 the religious settlement amounted to 'a severe defeat for the restored monarchy, and one which Charles deeply resented'.[36]

By the end of 1665 three other pieces of legislation ensured that the restored church became yet more intolerant: the Quaker Act of 1662 put in place severe penalties for those who attended separatist conventicles or refused to swear the Oath of Allegiance; all meetings of five or more people held 'under colour or pretence of any exercise of religion' were declared illegal by the Conventicle Act of 1664, and the Five Mile Act of 1665 prohibited those ministers ejected according to the terms of the Act of Uniformity from coming within five miles of their former parish or any city or borough. In 1668 Charles sponsored schemes for toleration and comprehension but, as in 1662, met intense hostility from parliament which led to their defeat. Ominously, when the king let the Conventicle Act expire without being renewed in 1668, the Commons refused to grant supply until Charles gave his assent to a new act. The resulting Conventicle Act of 1670 was considerably more draconian than its predecessor. One tract argued that it was an imposition upon the king since it was 'expressly against . . . [his] printed Declarations and Promises for Indulgence'.[37]

Charles's ambition to fashion a magnanimous religious settlement was thus thwarted, though the crown–parliament duality should not be overstressed. Tim Harris notes that 'MPs were more divided than is usually recognised' and that the Anglican measures 'were successful only after extremely close votes'.[38] A significant minority in the Lords seems to have been supportive of the sort of church that Charles sought to establish. Moreover, the monarch's right to dispense occasional individuals from compliance with certain statutes was not seriously questioned. Nevertheless, there is no doubt that the royal will had been curbed. In response, Charles sought to establish liberty of conscience other than through parliament, but his attempt to do so polarised opinion and induced a debate about the royal prerogative.

After 1670 Charles had another compelling motive for wanting to bring the dissenters within the national church. Having allied with France in 1670 (the Treaty of Dover) he was henceforth preparing to fight against the Dutch. In order to dissuade the dissenters from colluding with their fellow Protestants across the Channel – thereby acting as a fifth column – it was more important than ever that he should mitigate the penal laws against them. Thus in 1672 Charles issued the Declaration of Indulgence, dispensing with ecclesiastical statutes by royal prerogative on the basis 'that supreme power in ecclesiastical matters . . . is not only inherent in us but hath been declared and recognised to be so by several statutes and Acts of Parliament'.[39] Probably in the hope of uniting the dissenters and Catholics against the Anglican establishment, all penal laws against both groups were henceforth suspended. But this action forced a debate on what was a grey area of the prerogative, for it was generally accepted that the crown could use its prerogative only to dispense individuals, not large numbers of men, from the law. The king's claim that he was acting in accordance with the Act of Supremacy was met with the Anglican retort that the supremacy belonged not to the crown alone, but to the crown-in-parliament.

A considerable number of dissenters, like the Anglicans, regarded the Indulgence as illegal. Nevertheless, most seem to have availed themselves of the toleration it offered, in the process explicitly defending the king's prerogative to suspend ecclesiastical laws.

The Indulgence thus brought out into the open the extraordinary alteration in allegiances that had been taking place since 1660. However, when the war effort obliged Charles to seek supply from parliament, the price of members' monetary assistance was the cancellation of the Indulgence and royal assent to the Test Act in 1673 (see p. 79). Parliament had once again curbed the ambitions of the crown. Since the Test Act had revealed James as a Catholic, bills were now proposed in the Lords to secure the Protestant religion. One of these stipulated that James could not remarry (his first wife, Anne Hyde, had died in 1671) without the approval of parliament, the penalty for breach of which was to be exclusion from the succession. Another insisted that any children that James might have in the future were to be brought up as Protestants. So great an invasion of the royal prerogative did these bills threaten that Charles was forced to prorogue parliament.

Parliament appeared not only to have restrained the crown but also to have reformed it when, out of the rubble left behind by the collapse of the Cabal (see p. 79), emerged Danby, a career politician committed to the Church of England and opposed to religious toleration for either dissenters or Catholics. When members of parliament assembled in April 1675, Charles informed them that he would 'leave nothing undone that may show any zeal to the Protestant religion, as it is established in the Church of England from which I will never depart'.[40] However, Charles's obvious sympathies to the Catholics, combined with the fact that the Test Act had revealed the heir to the throne as a Catholic, encouraged many members of parliament to fear popery more than the dissenters. This explains why, when Danby introduced a test bill in parliament in 1675 – which required all office-holders and members of parliament to swear an oath which committed them not to seek the alteration of government in either church or state and forbade them in any way to resist royal authority – it was perceived by many members as an attempt to establish absolute and arbitrary government. Above all, it would have cemented the hegemony of the Anglican interest at a time when many considered it necessary to win the support of the dissenters in order to thwart what appeared to be an increasingly ominous popish menace. Indeed, to many observers Danby's style of government and his indifference to private conscience smacked of 'popery', an anxiety that was famously articulated by Marvell in his tract *An account of the growth of popery and arbitrary government* (see p. 80).

These were the conditions which brought the talented Shaftesbury into the open as spokesman for the Country opposition and, in the short term, ensured the defeat of the Test Bill in 1675. Religiously inspired opposition had once again prevented the government from implementing its will. More importantly, Danby's policies were directly responsible for ensuring that the vast majority of the political nation once again came to fear Catholicism more than the radical Protestantism associated with many of the dissenters. Only against this background is it possible to understand the Exclusion Crisis and the extraordinary assault launched during those years (1678–81) by the Whigs upon the crown prerogative, examined in the last section.

It is worth stressing that religion was a key source of division between the Whigs and the Tories during the Exclusion Crisis. It determined the nature of the party struggle of these years. On the one hand, the Whigs championed the cause of dissent against the intolerance of the Anglicans and sought to secure the liberties of Protestants not only under a future Catholic monarch but also under Charles II. By definition, this meant invading the crown prerogative. On the other hand, the Tories were defenders of the Anglican church, implacable enemies of dissent, and more concerned about the threat to public order posed by the Whigs and their dissenter allies than they were about the prospect of a popish successor. That exclusion failed was at least in part because religion had imbued each side with an ideological position which ensured that the crisis was very grave indeed, so grave that many of the political nation came to realise that they feared another civil war more than they feared the Tory–Anglicans. Thereafter, the Whig–dissenters were broken.

Religion under James II

Upon the accession of James II in 1685 it was therefore only the Tory–Anglicans who could have offered any resistance to the new king. Yet in 1685 the Tory–Anglicans remained intensely loyal to James, even though the Protestant Church of England had at its head a Catholic monarch. Wedded and glued to the principles of non-resistance and passive obedience, they placed loyalty to the legitimate succession above religious considerations. However, James's conduct (see pp. 82–83) undermined this loyalty to such an extent that it quickly became clear that he could not realistically expect this element to provide religious toleration for the Catholics, the overriding ambition of the king. He thus determined to form an alliance with the dissenters 'in the hope that the disabilities under which they suffered would give them common cause with the Catholics to support the removal of the penal laws'.[41] By relieving them from the terms of the test and corporation acts, this element would be eligible to sit in a future parliament and, duly grateful to the king – or, at least, so James reasoned – they would henceforth overturn the statutory authority of the test and corporation acts.

Therefore, on 4 April 1687 James issued a Declaration of Indulgence that suspended the test and corporation acts, as well as the penal laws, against Catholics and dissenters.[42] For these laws to be abrogated in this way by an openly Catholic king represented a direct threat to the Anglican establishment. Moreover, many – including those who benefited from the Indulgence – considered James's action to be an abuse of the prerogative. After all, the use of the prerogative to suspend penal laws in religious matters had already twice been declared illegal by the Commons, in 1663 and 1673. Thus, Anglicans and dissenters made common cause as Protestants against the spectre of rampant popery, the exact opposite of what James had intended.

James now made a series of mistakes which led directly to the Glorious Revolution. Allowing himself to believe that his policy was in fact working, on 27 April 1688 he reissued the Declaration of Indulgence and ordered that it be read from the pulpits of all Anglican churches. This was akin to leaving a political prisoner in a cell with a loaded gun and expecting him to do the 'decent thing'. However, the archbishop of Canterbury and six other bishops refused to do what was expected of them. Instead, they presented a petition to James demanding that he withdraw his order that they should publicly read the declaration on the grounds that 'it was founded upon such a dispensing power as hath often been declared illegal in Parliament'.[43] Regarding this action as a 'standard of rebellion', James had the bishops tried on a charge of seditious libel, only to be further outraged when they were acquitted – to popular rejoicing.

Until now James's Protestant subjects had at least been able to look forward to a Protestant successor, the king's Protestant daughter, Mary, from his first marriage. When the queen gave birth to a son, thereby raising the prospect of a Catholic dynasty, seven leading Protestants – five Whigs, two Tories – wrote a letter to William of Orange, the husband of Mary. It amounted to an invitation to invade. William landed at Torbay in south-west England on 5 November 1688 and prepared to engage in battle. James had joined his soldiers at Salisbury, but his nerve broke and he fled back to London. After an unsuccessful attempt to leave for the continent, he was permitted by William to make his way safely to France. The Glorious Revolution was under way.

Document case study

The Declarations of Indulgence and reactions to them

5.1 The king's reply on 24 February 1673 to the Commons' address of 14 February 1673, requesting him to withdraw the Declaration of Indulgence

His Majesty hath received an Address from you . . . and returneth this answer.

That he is very much troubled that that Declaration [of Indulgence], which he put out for ends so necessary to the quiet of his kingdom . . . should have proved the cause of disquiet in his House of Commons, and give occasion to the questioning of his power in ecclesiastics [= church affairs] which he finds not done in the reigns of any of his ancestors. He is sure he never had thoughts of using it otherwise than as it hath been entrusted in him, to the peace and establishment of the Church of England, and the ease of all his subjects in general. Neither did he pretend [= claim] the right of suspending any laws wherein the properties, rights or liberties of any of his subjects are concerned; nor to alter anything in the established doctrine or discipline of the Church of England, but his only design in this was to take off the penalties the statutes inflict upon Dissenters.

Source: *Commons' journals*, vol. 9, p. 256, reprinted in J. P. Kenyon (ed.), *The Stuart Constitution: documents and commentary*, 2nd edition, Cambridge, 1986, pp. 383–84.

5.2 From the Commons' answer, 26 February 1673

We find that the said answer is not sufficient to clear the apprehensions that may justly remain in the minds of your people, by your Majesty's having claimed a power to suspend penal statutes in matters ecclesiastical . . . [which was] never questioned in the reigns of any of your ancestors. Wherein we humbly conceive your Majesty hath been very much misinformed, since no such power was ever claimed or exercised by any of your Majesty's predecessors; and if it should be admitted might tend to the interrupting of the free course of the laws, and altering the legislative power, which hath always been acknowledged to reside in your Majesty and your two Houses of Parliament.

Source: *Commons' journals*, vol. 9, p. 257, reprinted in Kenyon (ed.), *Stuart Constitution*, p. 384.

5.3 From the Declaration of Indulgence, 4 April 1687

We therefore, out of our princely care and affection unto all our loving subjects, that they may live at ease and quiet, and for the increase of trade and encouragement of strangers, have thought fit by virtue of our royal prerogative to issue forth this our Declaration of Indulgence, making no doubt of the concurrence of our two Houses of Parliament when we shall think it convenient for them to meet.

In the first place we do declare that we will protect and maintain our archbishops, bishops and clergy, and all other our subjects of the Church of England in the free exercise of their religion as by law established, and in the quiet and full enjoyment of all their possessions, without any molestation or disturbance whatsoever.

We do likewise declare that it is our royal will and pleasure that from henceforth the execution of all and all manner of penal laws in matters ecclesiastical, for not coming to church, or not receiving the sacrament, or for any other nonconformity to the religion established, or for or by reason of the exercise of religion in any manner whatsoever, be immediately suspended; and the further execution of the said penal laws and every of them is hereby suspended.

Source: Edward Cardwell (ed.), *Documentary annals of the reformed Church of England*, 2 vols., Oxford, 1844, vol. 2, pp. 359–63, reprinted in Kenyon (ed.), *Stuart Constitution*, pp. 389–91.

5.4 From the Petition of the Seven Bishops, 18 May 1688

The great averseness they find in themselves in the distributing and publishing in all their churches your Majesty's late Declaration for liberty of conscience proceeds . . . especially [from the consideration that] that Declaration, if founded upon such a dispensing power as hath been often declared illegal in Parliament, and particularly in the years 1662–3 and 1672–3, . . . [then] your petitioners cannot in prudence, honour or conscience so far make themselves parties to it as the distribution of it all over the nation, and the solemn publication of it once and again even in God's house.

Source: Cardwell (ed.), *Annals*, vol. 2, pp. 367–70, reprinted in Kenyon (ed.), *Stuart Constitution*, pp. 406–7.

5.5 From the letter of invitation to William of Orange, 30 June 1688

The people [here] are so generally dissatisfied with the present conduct of the government in relation to their religion, liberties and properties (all of which have been greatly invaded) . . . that your Highness may be assured there are nineteen parts of twenty of the people throughout the kingdom who are desirous of a change, and who, we believe, would willingly contribute to it . . . It is no less certain that much the greatest part of the nobility and gentry are as much dissatisfied . . . and there is no doubt but that some of the most considerable of them would venture themselves with your Highness at your first landing . . . [Moreover] we do much doubt whether this present state of things will not yet be much changed to the worse before another year . . . by such other changes as are . . . to be expected from a packed Parliament.

Source: Sir John Dalrymple, *Memoirs of Great Britain and Ireland*, 3 vols., Edinburgh, 1771–8, App. 1, pp. 228–31, reprinted in Andrew Browning (ed.), *English historical documents, 1660–1714*, London, 1953, vol. 8, pp. 120–22.

Document case-study questions

1 Comment on the following phrases:
   (a) 'no such power was ever claimed or exercised by any of your Majesty's predecessors' (5.2);
   (b) 'often declared illegal in Parliament' (5.4);
   (c) 'religion, liberties and properties (all of which have been greatly invaded)' (5.5);
   (d) 'a packed Parliament' (5.5).

2 Read 5.1. What can be inferred from this source about the ways in which the Commons have criticised the Declaration of Indulgence?

3 In the light of 5.2, why were the Commons particularly alarmed by 5.3, the Declaration of Indulgence of 1687?

4 Read 5.3. Referring to tone and content, explain how James attempted to head off criticism.

5 Use these sources and your own knowledge to assess how far William could rely upon assurances made in 5.5.

Notes and references

1 Quoted in David L. Smith, *A history of the modern British Isles, 1603–1707: the double crown*, Oxford, 1998, p. 201.

2 Quoted in Smith, *History*, pp. 203–4.

3 Quoted in Maurice Ashley, *Charles II*, London, 1973, p. 12.

4 J. P. Kenyon, *The Stuarts*, London, 1958, p. 116.

5 Quoted in Smith, *History*, p. 201.

6 These lines are taken from *A satire on Charles II* (1697) by John Wilmot, earl of Rochester. It can be found in Alastair Fowler (ed.), *Seventeenth century verse*, Oxford, 1991, pp. 760–61.

7 Antonia Fraser, *Charles II*, London, 1979, p. 285.

8 Quoted in Smith, *History*, p. 226.

9 Quoted in W. A. Speck, *Reluctant revolutionaries: Englishmen and the revolution of 1688*, Oxford, 1988, p. 42.

10 Quoted in Speck, *Reluctant revolutionaries*, p. 43.

11 Quoted in John Miller, *James II: a study in kingship*, Hove, 1978, p. 126.

12 Quoted in Miller, *James II*, p. 127.

13 Quoted in Speck, *Reluctant revolutionaries*, p. 121.

14 Quoted in Miller, *James II*, p. 123.

15 Quoted in Miller, *James II*, p. 235.

16 See John Miller, *An English absolutism? The later Stuart monarchy 1660–1688*, London, 1993.

17 Quoted in Roger Lockyer, *Tudor and Stuart Britain, 1471–1714*, 2nd edition, Harlow, 1985, p. 341.

18 Quoted in Tim Harris, *Politics under the later Stuarts: party conflict in a divided society*, Harlow, 1993, p. 56.

19 Quoted in J. P. Kenyon (ed.), *The Stuart Constitution: documents and commentary*, 2nd edition, Cambridge, 1986, p. 363.

20 Kenyon (ed.), *Stuart Constitution*, p. 363.

21 Quoted in Geoffrey Holmes, *The making of a great power: late Stuart and early Georgian Britain 1660–1722*, Harlow, 1993, p. 117.

22 Quoted in Smith, *History*, p. 235.

23 Holmes, *The making of a great power*, p. 116.

24 Quoted in Holmes, *The making of a great power*, p. 117.

25 Holmes, *The making of a great power*, p. 117.

26 Quoted in Smith, *History*, p. 253.

27 John Miller, 'The later Stuart monarchy', in J. R. Jones (ed.), *The restored monarchy 1660–1688*, London, 1979, p. 43.

28 John Morrill, *Stuart Britain: a very short introduction*, Oxford, 2000, p. 74.

29 Quoted in Holmes, *The making of a great power*, p. 172.

30 Quoted in David Ogg, *England in the reigns of James II and William III*, Oxford, 1984, p. 510.

31 Quoted in Tim Harris, *Politics under the later Stuarts*, p. 69.

32 Quoted in Harris, *Politics under the later Stuarts*, p. 45.

33 For the full text of the Declaration of Breda see Kenyon (ed.), *Stuart Constitution*, pp. 331–32.

34 For these acts see Kenyon (ed.), *Stuart Constitution*, pp. 351–56.

35 Harris, *Politics under the later Stuarts*, p. 69.

36 R. A. Beddard, 'The Restoration church', in J. R. Jones (ed.), *The restored monarchy*, pp. 165–66.

37 Quoted in Harris, *Politics under the later Stuarts*, p. 68.

38 Harris, *Politics under the later Stuarts*, pp. 44–45.

39 See Kenyon (ed.), *Stuart Constitution*, pp. 382–83.

40 Quoted in Smith, *History*, p. 232.

41 Harris, *Politics under the later Stuarts*, p. 126.

42 For the text of this Indulgence, see Kenyon (ed.), *Stuart Constitution*, pp. 389–91.

43 Quoted in Smith, *History*, p. 281.

6

The position in 1689

The monarchy: nature and powers

By 1689 much had changed in the English polity. The central institutions outwardly still resembled those of 1558; the crown, the privy council, parliament, the law courts and the Church of England remained at the heart of government. Yet behind this superficial continuity, much about the nature and role of these structures had altered in the 131 years since Elizabeth's accession. In particular, their respective powers and their relationship to each other differed very significantly from those described in the opening chapter of this book. This final chapter will discuss the nature of those changes and examine the extent to which they constituted the development of a more limited kind of monarchy.

In 1558 contemporaries had described the powers of the crown as both 'absolute' and 'legally limited'. One of the major consequences of the two revolutions of the seventeenth century was that by 1689 the monarchy had ceased to be regarded as 'absolute', and that term had instead become associated with tyranny and despotism. This shift was neatly summed up by the lord chancellor, John Somers, who in 1689 argued that:

> Our kings must act by law and not absolutely . . . So that our government not being arbitrary, but legal, not absolute, but political, our princes can never become arbitrary, absolute, or tyrants without forfeiting at the same time their royal character, by the breach of the essential customs of their regal power, which are to act according to the ancient customs and standing laws of the nation.[1]

Whereas Tudor and early Stuart writers had spoken of the monarchy as 'absolute' and 'legally limited' without any sense of contradiction, Somers spoke of 'absolute, arbitrary and tyrannical government' in a single breath as the antithesis of legal, constitutional monarchy. In the Revolution Settlement that was created after James II's departure it was this principle of a legally limited monarchy that was enshrined in a series of statutes.

The settlement was carefully constructed to attract support from all but the most extreme Tories and Whigs. It was sufficiently vague to offer a 'lowest common denominator' that the large middle ground of moderate opinion could accept. After lengthy debate, and despite initial opposition from a majority in the Lords, parliament resolved that James II had 'violated the fundamental laws; and having withdrawn himself out of this kingdom has abdicated the government;

and that the throne is thereby vacant'.[2] This form of words was vague enough to allow for a number of different interpretations of what had happened in 1688. Tories could believe that James's departure had led to William and Mary becoming *de facto* sovereigns, but they did not have to acknowledge them as the 'lawful and rightful' monarchs. Whigs, on the other hand, were free to believe that James had violated his contract and had been removed for that reason, and that the new monarchs were now bound by a contract. The key documents of the Revolution Settlement, especially the Bill of Rights and the new Coronation Oath, consciously avoided statements that would have been problematic for either Whigs or Tories to accept, and concentrated instead on statements that commanded the agreement of all but minorities at each end of the political spectrum.

The legal limits on royal powers were affirmed in the revised Coronation Oath which William and Mary took in 1689. Although the ceremonial of the coronation ceremony on 11 April 1689 remained traditional, the wording of the oath contained some highly significant changes.[3] Whereas James II and his predecessors had sworn to 'confirm to the people of England the laws and customs to them granted by the Kings of England', William and Mary swore to 'govern the people of England, according to the statutes in Parliament agreed on, and the laws and customs of the same'.[4] Although in one sense this changed rhetoric merely recognised the supremacy of statute that had long been constitutional reality, at another level it marked an important symbolic abandonment of the idea that the monarch was the creator of law. Instead, the monarchs explicitly acknowledged that everyone, themselves included, was subject to the rule of statute law.

The legal constraints on the crown's powers were systematically recited in February 1689 in the Declaration of Rights, which was enacted in statutory form at the end of that year in the Bill of Rights. Technically, neither document constituted a formal contract between William and Mary and their subjects. Indeed, on 13 February 1689 they were formally offered the throne *before* the declaration was read to them, and their proclamation as king and queen the next day was not made dependent upon their acceptance of the declaration. William had indeed made it clear that he 'would not take the crown upon conditions'.[5] Nevertheless, the Bill of Rights was passed as a statute and like all other statutes it received the royal assent. The bill could of course be amended or repealed by a subsequent statute. But in the meantime William and Mary had consented to it, and it could be cited in the law courts if the monarchs transgressed it.

The Bill of Rights curtailed royal powers in a number of highly significant ways. Among its most important provisions were a clause stating that the royal power of suspending laws 'without consent of Parliament is illegal', and another stipulating that the royal dispensing power 'as it hath been assumed and exercised of late is illegal'.[6] Whereas the first of these clauses completely ruled out the monarch's capacity to suspend any statute without parliamentary consent, the second was clearly directed at the excessive use that James II had made of the dispensing power during his brief reign. The monarch's powers in

Romeyn de Hooghe's engraving of the coronation of William and Mary on 11 April 1689.

relation to statutes were thus significantly curtailed, and although the royal power to veto legislation remained intact, and has never been formally abolished, it was used for the last time by Queen Anne in 1708.

Another clause in the Bill of Rights confirmed the abolition of prerogative sources of revenue that had taken place in the 1640s and been confirmed at the Restoration in 1660. It stated that 'the levying [of] money for or to the use of the crown, by pretence of prerogative, without grant of Parliament, for longer time, or in other manner than the same is or shall be granted, is illegal'. This affirmed the crown's financial dependence upon parliament and thereby greatly strengthened the parliamentary 'power of the purse'. This was a crucial development at a time when England was embarking on a quarter-century of almost continuous and highly expensive wars against France: the Nine Years' War (1689–97) and then the War of the Spanish Succession (1702–13). It was symptomatic of a fundamentally changed relationship between crown and parliament, the nature of which is worth exploring in detail.

The role of parliament

The Revolution Settlement of 1689 ushered in a new period in the history of the English parliament. The fact that parliament was now financially indispensable to the crown ensured that it became a permanent institution of government, and it is a remarkable fact that a parliament has met in England every year since 1689. It thus became, for the first time, an institution rather than an event. The Bill of Rights stated that 'for redress of all grievances, and for the amending, strengthening and preserving of the laws, parliaments ought to be held frequently', and in 1694 the Triennial Act (stronger and easier to enforce than those of 1641 or 1664) required that 'henceforth a Parliament shall be holden once in three years at the least'.[7] But what really ensured that these statements became a reality was the fact that the Revolution Settlement deliberately left the crown financially dependent upon parliament. Under James II parliament had learned the hard way what happened when a monarch had enough revenue not to need parliamentary grants. By 1689, Whigs and Tories alike were determined that this should never be the case again. The Whig William Sacheverell urged the Commons in January 1689 to 'secure this House, that Parliaments be duly chosen and not kicked out at pleasure, which never could have been done without such an extravagant revenue that they might never stand in need of Parliaments'. Similarly, the following year a Tory, Paul Foley, argued that 'if we settle such a revenue as that the King should have no need of a parliament, I think we do not our duty to them that sent us hither'.[8] As Gilbert Burnet put it, 'it was taken up as a general maxim, that a revenue for a certain and short term, was the best security that the nation could have frequent Parliaments'.[9] These feelings led parliament to grant William an annual revenue capped at £1.2 million, half of which was to be used for civil administration and the other half to fund military campaigns. William complained that 'the Commons used him like a dog',[10] but his determination to bring England into the continental war against Louis XIV meant that parliament had him over a barrel.

The grant of a fixed annual revenue to the crown also sounded the final death-knell of the antiquated financial system, based on the distinction between the crown's ordinary and extraordinary revenues, which had existed since the fourteenth century. The inadequacies of these arrangements had become ever more glaring during the course of the seventeenth century. Instead, a new system emerged in which royal government was financed by annual parliamentary grants, known from 1698 as the Civil List. Virtually all public revenues came to depend on parliamentary consent, and the proportion of national funds derived from non-parliamentary sources declined from 76 per cent in 1626–40 to 10 per cent in 1661–85, and to only 3 per cent by 1689–1714.[11] The crown became in effect a department of state, funded like all other departments by parliament. The personal revenues of the monarch became subsumed within a national financial system whose credit rested on parliamentary guarantees.

These developments went along with much tighter parliamentary control over the spending of the revenues that it granted. The principle of 'appropriation' –

briefly attempted in 1624, the mid-1660s and the late 1670s – became firmly established in the years immediately after 1689, ensuring that parliamentary supply could only be used for the specific purpose for which it had been voted. Parliament also made increasing use of the device of 'tacking', whereby political demands were 'tacked' on to revenue bills. More and more, the government's financial conduct and probity were subject to parliamentary scrutiny, and in 1690 the Commons established the Commission of Public Accounts to monitor expenditure, enforce 'appropriation' and investigate mismanagement.

This changed financial relationship between crown and parliament, together with his desperate need for wartime revenue, meant that William was in no position to resist other constitutional reforms which strengthened parliament's powers and diminished those of the monarch. As well as stating that parliaments 'ought to be held frequently', the Bill of Rights enshrined the principle of parliamentary freedom of speech in statute for the first time, declaring that 'the freedom of speech, and debates or proceedings in Parliament, ought not to be impeached or questioned in any court or place out of Parliament'. A privilege that had hitherto still technically rested on royal grant in response to the speaker's supplication thus became guaranteed by statute. In a further clause clearly prompted by James II's attempt to pack parliament, the bill also stipulated that 'election of members of parliament ought to be free', thereby giving this freedom a statutory basis for the first time.

Another important new parliamentary constraint upon royal action was the clause in the Bill of Rights that 'the raising or keeping [of] a standing army within the kingdom in time of peace, unless it be with consent of Parliament, is against law'. Once again prompted by the recent experiences of James II's reign, this was a further encroachment on what had long been regarded as one of the crown's prerogatives. This reform was further reinforced by the 1689 Mutiny Act, which confirmed the need for parliament to consent to any standing army in peacetime and also made the punishment of mutiny and the authority to hold courts martial dependent on statute. Since the relevant statute was only passed for a specified period of time, this gave parliament considerable control over military discipline when the act expired.

All these changes set the course for crown–parliament relations over the years that followed. Royal freedom of action in a variety of spheres was defined by statute and made subject to parliamentary review. In 1701, the Act of Settlement (which will be discussed again in the following sections) even circumscribed the monarch's control over foreign policy by requiring that if the monarch was not 'a native of this kingdom of England', then the nation would not 'be obliged to engage in any war for the defence of any dominions or territories which do not belong to the Crown of England, without the consent of Parliament'.[12] More and more, the mechanism of statute regulated and limited royal powers to a greater extent than ever before, providing a legally enforceable means of controlling the idiosyncrasies and whims of individual monarchs. There was a gradual diminution of the monarch's powers in relation to parliament. A further symptom of this trend was the fact that from 1695 onwards the speaker of the Commons ceased to be a crown nominee and was instead nominated by whichever party had a majority in the house. Whereas in 1558 parliament had been an agency of royal government and an extension of the conciliar structures that surrounded the crown, by 1689 it was coming to resemble a watchdog over the king and a means of restricting his freedom of action. This shift was also evident, albeit in a more muted form, in parliament's relationship with the privy council and the crown's appointment of advisers.

The privy council and royal advisers

During the 1640s, the Houses of Parliament had made the unprecedented demand that they should have the right to approve the king's appointments of privy councillors and other officers of state. In the later years of the Civil War, this demand was extended into the right of parliamentary nomination to those offices. There was no attempt to revive such demands at the Restoration, or after the revolution of 1688–89, and the monarch's right to appoint privy councillors and other officers of state remained intact. Nevertheless, certain reforms were enacted which introduced a greater separation between parliament and the body of royal advisers and officials than had existed in the middle of the sixteenth century.

After 1689 there was a growing belief that parliamentary scrutiny of the government's conduct, especially in fiscal matters, would be compromised if certain officials were members of parliament. Between 1694 and 1706, a series of 'place clauses' were 'tacked' onto various revenue bills to exclude several thousand office-holders from sitting in parliament. The device of tacking was adopted after William vetoed a place bill intended to counter 'the secret advices of particular persons who may have private interests of their own'.[13] These requirements were further reinforced by a clause in the Act of Settlement which stated that 'no person who has an office or place of profit under the King, or receives a pension from the crown, shall be capable of serving as a member of the House of Commons'.[14] The effect of this was to begin to create a distinction between the executive and the legislature of a kind that had not existed previously.

This 'place' legislation was accompanied by attempts to counter the advice of 'hidden' advisers. These were private individuals who were not members of the privy council and possibly did not even hold major state office, but who nevertheless had the monarch's confidence and were secretly consulted on a range of important matters. The Tudors and Stuarts had all made extensive use of such informal advisers at various times. It was this practice that the Act of Settlement sought to curtail when it stated that 'all matters and things relating to the well governing of this kingdom, which are properly cognizable in the Privy Council by the laws and customs of this realm, shall be transacted there'.[15] This attempted to regulate the monarch's use of unofficial advisers in a way that was unprecedented.

The years after 1689 also saw a significant change in the nature of the privy council. For much of the 1690s, William spent extended periods of time away leading military campaigns on the continent. Until her death in 1694, Mary deputised for him during these absences, and to make executive government more effective an inner circle known as the 'Cabinet Council' began to emerge within the privy council. This was able to conduct business more efficiently than a full council, which had become too large in its membership. The term 'Cabinet Council', first used in the 1630s, henceforth became common usage, and this body was the ancestor of the modern cabinet. These years thus saw the beginnings of the separation of the privy council and the cabinet into two distinct institutions, a separation that still exists today. This marked another stage in the constant process of evolution and adaptation that had been going on intermittently since the 1530s.

Law courts and the rule of law

The Revolution Settlement emphasised the legally limited nature of the monarchy, and this was naturally reflected in a changed relationship between the crown's powers and the rule of law. The monarchy's relations with the law courts and the judiciary were similarly altered. The Bill of Rights contained a series of allegations that James II had acted illegally, most notably by: 'prosecutions in the Court of King's Bench, for matters and causes cognizable only in Parliament; and by divers other arbitrary and illegal courses'; by allowing 'partial, corrupt, and unqualified persons' to serve as jurors; by requiring 'excessive bail . . . of persons committed in criminal cases, to elude the benefit of the laws made for the liberty of the subjects'; and by imposing 'excessive fines' and 'illegal and cruel punishments'. All of these matters were then systematically addressed in the bill and in other statutes in the years immediately afterwards.

First of all, the bill required that 'jurors ought to be duly impanelled and returned', and that jurors in 'trials for high treason ought to be freeholders'. Likewise, 'excessive bail' was not to be required, and 'excessive fines' and 'cruel and unusual punishments' were not to be imposed. Cases cognizable in parliament had to be tried there and not transferred to other courts. These stipulations were confirmed and amplified by the Trial of Treasons Act (1696). This statute also ensured that the scales were less heavily weighted against those accused of treason by stating that they were to receive a copy of the indictment at least five days before their trial, that they could swear witnesses in their own defence, and that a conviction needed more than one witness for the prosecution.[16] All these measures regularised the conduct of treason trials and reduced the scope for the crown to push through a conviction for treason without a fair and careful hearing.

The monarch's powers in relation to the judiciary were also diminished during this period. Hitherto, judges had held tenure only during the monarch's pleasure (*durante bene placito*) and could thus be removed at will. Most monarchs were relatively restrained in their use of this power. Charles II, for example, had sacked

11 judges during the last 9 years of his reign. James II, by contrast, removed no fewer than 18 judges in less than 3 years, and such behaviour prompted demands that the terms of judges' tenure should be changed. A statement in the Bill of Rights that they should be appointed 'for as long as they shall do good' (*quamdiu se bene gesserint*) was removed at William's request, and he vetoed a bill to this effect in 1692. However, in practice he never violated this principle, and the Act of Settlement stated plainly that 'judges' commissions be made *quamdiu se bene gesserint*'. It was however added that 'upon the address of both Houses of Parliament it may be lawful to remove them'.[17] Judges could thus not be removed unilaterally by the monarch, but they could be removed at parliament's request. Once again, parliament was gaining powers at the expense of the crown. This change in judges' tenure also had the effect of making the judiciary more independent of the monarch. Just as we saw above that by the 1690s a growing divergence was opening up between executive and legislature, so the judiciary made a significant step away from dependence on the crown. The organic system of government so characteristic of the 'body politic' in 1558 was by 1689 giving way to one based on 'checks and balances' and a 'separation of powers'.

Religion and the church

We saw in the opening chapter that the religious history of mid-sixteenth-century England offered an excellent illustration of the principle adopted at the League of Augsburg in 1555, that the religion of the nation followed that of the monarch (*cuius regio eius religio*). Strongly Protestant under Edward VI, strongly Catholic under Mary I, and then moderately Protestant under Elizabeth, Tudor England broadly followed the faith of the reigning monarch. The monarchs were entirely free to choose their own faith, and that choice had a direct impact on their subjects' religious practices.

However, by 1689 this picture had changed dramatically. During the course of the seventeenth century, the principle of *cuius regio eius religio* had been gradually eroded. Charles I, and even more spectacularly James II, found that they could not simply impose their own religious preferences on their subjects. In that sense, the Elizabethan Settlement had tied the hands of Elizabeth's successors. It had established a broad, inclusive and generally tolerant church that remained in existence after her death. One of the biggest sources of political instability during the Stuart period was the fear that certain monarchs were at best lukewarm in their support of the established church and were seeking either to undermine it or to push it in a more 'popish' direction. There was thus a tension between the royal supremacy, re-established in 1559, and the Protestant character of the church. To what extent could the monarch fundamentally alter the established church? This in turn had important political implications, for in English eyes Catholicism was widely associated with royal authoritarianism. 'Popery and arbitrary government' came to be spoken of in the same breath, and such fears contributed greatly to the profound mistrust which Charles I and James II in particular inspired in many of their subjects.

The 1689 Revolution Settlement ushered in a new era by introducing a fundamentally important reform. The Bill of Rights stated that 'it hath been found by experience that it is inconsistent with the safety and welfare of this Protestant kingdom, to be governed by a popish prince, or by any King or Queen marrying a papist'. It therefore requested that any Catholic, or anyone married to a Catholic, should henceforth be 'for ever incapable to inherit, possess, or enjoy the crown and government of this realm and Ireland'. This marked a complete reversal of the principle of *cuius regio eius religio*; henceforth, the religion of the nation would determine the religion of the monarch, not the other way round.

This reversal was also evident in the revised Coronation Oath. Whereas James II and all his predecessors had sworn in very general terms to 'keep peace and godly agreement entirely according to [their] power, to the holy Church, the clergy and the people', and to protect the 'Churches committed to [their] charge', William and Mary swore to 'maintain the laws of God, the true profession of the gospel, and the Protestant reformed religion established by law'.[18] The commitment to the established Protestant Church of England was thus made explicit. Here, as in other respects, the monarch's freedom was subordinated to the power of statute. This restriction was then affirmed by the 1701 Act of Settlement, which stated that 'whosoever shall hereafter come to the possession of this crown shall join in communion with the Church of England, as by law established'.[19]

This restriction of the monarch's personal faith, which remains in force to this day, was highly significant because it removed at a stroke one of the most troublesome sources of political instability that had dogged England since the Reformation. Ever since the royal supremacy had been established, the potential existed for the monarch's own religious beliefs to come into conflict with those of the established church. Fears that this was happening, or might happen, were recurrent sources of political mistrust, especially under the Stuarts. As John Morrill has written, 'the Stuarts would have been a happier dynasty if they had been able to embrace the Anglicanism of the majority of their people'.[20] The measures of 1689 and 1701 resolved this problem once and for all by *obliging* the monarch to embrace Anglicanism; here again, the monarch's personal freedom was restricted and explicitly subordinated to the power of statute.

Ironically, this curbing of the monarch's freedom was accompanied by a greater degree of religious toleration for the subjects. In 1689, a toleration act was passed that scaled down some of the penalties on Protestant dissenters enacted since the Restoration. The act was based on the premise that 'some ease to scrupulous consciences in the exercise of religion may be an effectual means to unite their Majesties' Protestant subjects in interest and affection'.[21] Although the Corporation Act (1661) and the Test Acts (1673 and 1678) remained in force, and dissenters were therefore still excluded from public office, they were henceforth allowed to worship freely, provided that they took the Oath of Allegiance to the monarch, made a declaration against the Catholic doctrine of transubstantiation, and had their meeting houses licensed by the civil or ecclesiastical authorities. Over 900 such meeting houses were licensed within a year, and only Catholics, Jews and Unitarians were excluded completely.

Despite its limitations, the Toleration Act did mark a recognition that the established church could no longer claim to be a national, inclusive church. Until that point, the Church of England had maintained the claim, inherited from medieval Catholicism, that it was the only legitimate church and could rightfully comprehend the whole realm. The Elizabethan Settlement of 1559 assumed that a subject was automatically a member of the church unless they deliberately opted out, which in practice relatively few chose to do. Under Elizabeth and James, these attempts at 'comprehension' met with some success. But Charles I's policies polarised religious opinion and spawned a radical opposition. At the Restoration, a narrow church settlement was established that imposed harsh penalties on those who refused to conform. Only in 1689 was it finally conceded that some people could legitimately worship outside the established church. As Mark Goldie has written, the Toleration Act 'marked the final exhaustion of the ideal of a single, national, Reformed Church, and the reluctant beginning of a permanent religious pluralism'.[22]

With this also went the erosion of the idea that the church and the state were coterminous, and that everyone owed allegiance to the monarch as supreme head of the church just as they owed secular allegiance to the head of state. Gradually the church became less effective as an arm of the state, and associated more with a particular constellation of political and religious attitudes. The picture of the Church of England as 'the Tory party at prayer' has its beginnings in this period. In a sense, the monarchs had thus lost in two ways: no longer able to choose their own religion, and obliged to be Anglicans themselves, they none the less ruled over subjects whose freedom was henceforth not restricted in that way.

Conclusions

In analysing all the changes that had taken place by 1689, or in the years immediately afterwards, it is of course important not to lose sight of the very considerable elements of continuity that survived. As in 1558, England was still a monarchy, republicanism remained weak, and an effective relationship between the monarch and the political elite continued to be crucial for political stability.

Yet much about that relationship had altered. We have seen that in a range of ways the freedom of action of the monarch was more restricted at the end of the period covered in this book than it had been at the beginning. These restrictions were mostly enacted by statute and enforced by parliament. They involved a significantly adjusted relationship between crown and parliament in which powers were transferred from the former to the latter. Parliament henceforth became a permanent part of government, meeting every year, and the crown's chronic financial needs became the best guarantee of parliament's indispensability.

In 1558, the highly personal nature of the English monarchy still contained strong echoes of the medieval polity. The monarch was the head of the body politic, and the system formed an organic whole in which all institutions locked together to make royal government more effective. The powers of the crown could thus be described as both 'absolute' and 'legally limited' without this seeming paradoxical. By 1689, a new system was emerging, characterised by constitutional checks and balances, in which the monarchy was no longer regarded as 'absolute' precisely because it was 'legally limited'. The powers of parliament and statutes acted as limits and counterweights to royal action, and a separation of powers was beginning to become visible between executive, legislature and judiciary. In 1558, echoes of the medieval polity still survived in such features of the personal monarchy as the fact that parliaments were called or dissolved at the monarch's will, or that judges only had tenure during the monarch's pleasure. The fiscal system, based on the distinction between the crown's 'ordinary' and 'extraordinary' revenues, was essentially unchanged since the fourteenth century. By the 1690s, on the other hand, parliaments existed independently of the crown, and enforced statutes that reduced the impact of individual monarchs' personalities on political and religious affairs. Royal government was funded by annual parliamentary grants that were 'appropriated' for specific purposes. Such developments pointed decisively towards the more mixed, constitutional monarchy of the future. Several decades would pass before William Blackstone wrote in 1765 that royal powers were 'checked and kept within due bounds' by the two Houses of Parliament.[23] But in the Revolution Settlement of 1689 and its immediate aftermath, the crucial steps towards such a limited monarchy had been taken.

Document case study

The Revolution Settlement and its aftermath

6.1 Parliament asserts the 'rights and liberties of the subject'

From the Bill of Rights, 1689

That the pretended power of suspending of laws, or the execution of laws, by regal authority, without consent of Parliament, is illegal.

That the pretended power of dispensing with laws, or the execution of laws, by regal authority, as it hath been assumed and exercised of late, is illegal . . .

That levying of money for or to the use of the crown, by pretence of prerogative, without grant of Parliament, for longer time, or in other manner than the same is or shall be granted, is illegal . . .

That the raising or keeping a standing army within the kingdom in time of peace, unless it be with consent of Parliament, is illegal . . .

That election of members of Parliament ought to be free.

That the freedom of speech, and debates or proceedings in Parliament, ought not to be impeached or questioned in any court or place out of Parliament.

That excessive bail ought not to be required, nor excessive fines imposed; nor cruel and unusual punishments inflicted.

That jurors ought to be duly impanelled and returned, and jurors which pass upon men in trials for high treason ought to be freeholders . . .

And that for redress of all grievances, and for the amending, strengthening and preserving of the laws, Parliaments ought to be held frequently.

Source: E. N. Williams (ed.), *The eighteenth century Constitution: documents and commentary*, Cambridge, 1960, pp. 28–29.

6.2 William and Mary swear to uphold the laws and the Church of England

From the new Coronation Oath, introduced in 1689

Archbishop: Will you solemnly promise and swear to govern the people of this kingdom of England, and the dominions thereunto belonging, according to the statutes in Parliament agreed on, and the laws and customs of the same?

King and Queen: I solemnly promise so to do . . .

Archbishop: Will you to the utmost of your power maintain the laws of God, the true profession of the gospel, and the Protestant reformed religion established by law? And will you preserve unto the bishops and clergy of this realm, and to the churches there committed to their charge, all such rights and privileges as by law do or shall appertain unto them, or any of them?

King and Queen: All this I promise to do.

Source: Williams (ed.), *Eighteenth century Constitution*, pp. 37–38.

6.3 William complains about the financial settlement

From Gilbert Burnet's account of William's reaction to parliament's decision to vote him a fixed annual revenue of £1.2 million

[William] expressed an earnest desire to have the revenue of the crown settled on him for life: he said he was not a king till that was done: without that, the title of a king was only a pageant . . . He was sure that the worst of all governments was a king without treasure and without power. But a jealousy was now infused into many, that he would grow arbitrary in his government, if he once had the revenue; and would strain for a high stretch of prerogative as soon as he was out of difficulties and necessities.

Source: John Miller, *The Glorious Revolution*, Harlow, 1983, p. 117.

6.4 Whig reflections on the English Constitution

From J. Trenchard and W. Moyle, An argument showing that a standing army is inconsistent with a free government, 1697

Our constitution is a limited mixed monarchy, where the king enjoys all the prerogatives necessary to the support of his dignity and the protection of his people and is only abridged from the power of injuring his own subjects . . . Lest the extraordinary power intrusted in the crown should lean towards arbitrary government, or the tumultuary licentiousness of the people should incline towards a democracy, the wisdom of our ancestors hath instituted a middle state, viz. of nobility, whose interest is to trim [= balance] this boat of our commonwealth . . . The excellence of this government consists in the due balance of the several constituent parts of it, for if either one of them should be too hard for the other two, there is an actual dissolution of the constitution; but whilst we can continue in our present condition, we may without vanity reckon ourselves the happiest people in the world.

Source: Miller, *Glorious Revolution*, pp. 113–14.

6.5 Further constraints are placed on the crown's powers

From the Act of Settlement, 1701; the full title of this statute was 'an act for the further limitation of the crown and better securing of the rights and liberties of the subject'

That whosoever shall hereafter come to the possession of this crown, shall join in communion with the Church of England, as by law established.

That in case the crown and imperial dignity of this realm shall hereafter come to any person, not being a native of this kingdom of England, this nation be not obliged to engage in any war for the defence of any dominions or territories which do not belong to the crown of England, without the consent of Parliament.

That no person who shall hereafter come to the possession of this crown, shall go out of the dominions of England, Scotland, or Ireland, without consent of Parliament.

That . . . all matters and things relating to the well governing of this kingdom, which are properly cognizable in the Privy Council by the laws and customs of this realm, shall be transacted there . . .

That no person who has an office or place of profit under the King, or receives a pension from the crown, shall be capable of serving as a member of the House of Commons.

That . . . judges' commissions be made *quamdiu se bene gesserint* [= for as long as they shall do good], and their salaries ascertained and established; but upon the address of both Houses of Parliament it may be lawful to remove them.

That no pardon under the great seal of England be pleadable to an impeachment by the Commons in Parliament . . .

The laws of England are the birthright of the people thereof, and all the Kings and Queens who shall ascend the throne of this realm ought to administer the government of the same according to the said laws, and all their officers and ministers ought to serve them respectively according to the same . . .

Source: Williams (ed.), *Eighteenth century Constitution*, pp. 59–60.

Document case-study questions

1 To what extent, and in what ways, does 6.1 impose limitations on royal actions?

2 Comment on the significance of the wording of 6.2.

3 What light does 6.3 shed on the importance of financial issues in shaping the Revolution Settlement?

4 How far does the situation described in 6.4 differ from that which had existed in 1558? Consider the significance of your answer.

5 What further limitations are placed on royal powers and actions in 6.5? Why were these limitations imposed?

6 Using these sources and your wider knowledge, comment on how far England had become a limited monarchy by 1701.

Notes and references

1 David L. Smith, *A history of the modern British Isles, 1603–1707: the double crown*, Oxford, 1998, p. 344.

2 Smith, *History of the modern British Isles*, pp. 288–89.

3 Lois G. Schwoerer, 'The coronation of William and Mary, April 11, 1689', in Lois G. Schwoerer (ed.), *The revolution of 1688–1689: changing perspectives*, Cambridge, 1992, pp. 107–30.

4 E. N. Williams (ed.), *The eighteenth century Constitution: documents and commentary*, Cambridge, 1960, p. 37.

5 David L. Smith, *The Stuart parliaments, 1603–1689*, London, 1999, p. 164.

6 The full text of the Bill of Rights is printed in Williams (ed.), *Eighteenth century Constitution*, pp. 26–33, from which this and other quotations in this chapter from the bill are taken.

7 Williams (ed.), *Eighteenth century Constitution*, p. 50.

8 For these two quotations, see John Miller, *The Glorious Revolution*, Harlow, 1983, pp. 40, 42.

9 Williams (ed.), *Eighteenth century Constitution*, p. 4.

10 Miller, *Glorious Revolution*, pp. 40–41.

11 Michael J. Braddick, *The nerves of state: taxation and the financing of the English state, 1558–1714*, Manchester, 1996, p. 13.

12 Williams (ed.), *Eighteenth century Constitution*, p. 59.

13 Smith, *Stuart parliaments*, p. 168.

14 Williams (ed.), *Eighteenth century Constitution*, p. 59.

15 Williams (ed.), *Eighteenth century Constitution*, p. 59.

16 Williams (ed.), *Eighteenth century Constitution*, pp. 53–56.

17 Williams (ed.), *Eighteenth century Constitution*, p. 59.

18 Williams (ed.), *Eighteenth century Constitution*, pp. 37–39.

19 Williams (ed.), *Eighteenth century Constitution*, p. 59.

20 John Morrill, 'Politics in an age of revolution, 1630–1690', in John Morrill (ed.), *The Oxford illustrated history of Tudor and Stuart Britain*, Oxford, 1996, p. 396.

21 The Toleration Act is printed in Williams (ed.), *Eighteenth century Constitution*, pp. 42–46 (quotation at p. 42).

22 Mark Goldie, 'The search for religious liberty, 1640–1690', in Morrill (ed.), *Oxford illustrated history*, p. 309.

23 Williams (ed.), *Eighteenth century Constitution*, p. 74.

Select bibliography

It is difficult to construct a bibliography on the theme of the development of limited monarchy in England between 1558 and 1689. The issues of monarchy and its place within the polity are deeply embedded in much of the vast literature on this period, and yet there are relatively few works specifically devoted to this theme. What follows is therefore intended as a guide to further reading. It is necessarily selective, but attempts to identify some of the salient works in which the problems discussed in this book can be studied further.

Primary sources

Three collections of documents are especially useful on these themes: G. R. Elton (ed.), *The Tudor Constitution*, 2nd edition, Cambridge, 1982; J. P. Kenyon (ed.), *The Stuart Constitution*, 2nd edition, Cambridge, 1986; and E. N. Williams (ed.), *The eighteenth century Constitution*, Cambridge, 1960. All these books also contain valuable commentaries that place the extracts in context and provide an excellent introduction to English constitutional history in this period.

Older collections that are still useful for the range of documents they contain are: G. W. Prothero (ed.), *Select statutes and other constitutional documents illustrative of the reigns of Elizabeth I and James I*, 4th edition, Oxford, 1913; J. R. Tanner (ed.), *Constitutional documents of the reign of James I*, Cambridge, 1930; S. R. Gardiner (ed.), *Constitutional documents of the puritan revolution, 1625–1660*, 3rd edition, Oxford, 1906; and W. C. Costin and J. S. Watson (eds.), *The law and working of the Constitution, vol. 1, 1660–1783*, 2nd edition, London, 1961.

General

The following books contain useful overviews covering all or part of this period. For both Tudor and Stuart history, see especially A. G. R. Smith, *The emergence of a nation state: the Commonwealth of England, 1529–1660*, 2nd edition, Harlow, 1997; and John Morrill (ed.), *The Oxford illustrated history of Tudor and Stuart Britain*, Oxford, 1996. For the sixteenth century, see: Mark Nicholls, *A history of the modern British Isles, 1529–1603: the two kingdoms*, Oxford, 1999; John Guy, *Tudor England*, Oxford, 1988; and Susan Brigden, *New worlds, lost worlds: the rule of the Tudors, 1485–1603*, London, 2000. For the seventeenth century, see: David L. Smith, *A history of the modern British Isles, 1603–1707: the double crown*, Oxford, 1998; Barry Coward, *The Stuart age: England, 1603–1714*, 2nd edition, Harlow, 1994; Mark Kishlansky, *A monarchy transformed: Britain, 1603–1714*, London, 1996; and Jonathan Scott, *England's troubles: seventeenth-century political instability in European context*, Cambridge, 2000.

The history of parliaments and their relationship with the crown is explored in: Jennifer Loach, *Parliament under the Tudors*, Oxford, 1991; Michael A. R. Graves, *The Tudor parliaments: crown, Lords and Commons, 1485–1603*, Harlow, 1985; and David L. Smith, *The Stuart parliaments, 1603–1689*, London, 1999. The history of the church is charted in S. Doran and C. Durston, *Princes, pastors and people: the church and religion in England, 1529–1689*, London, 1991.

Elizabeth I

In addition to the general works listed above, there is a fine survey of the reign in Penry Williams, *The later Tudors: England, 1547–1603*, Oxford, 1995. Two good recent biographies of Elizabeth, offering contrasting approaches and interpretations, are Christopher Haigh, *Elizabeth I*, Harlow, 1988; and Wallace MacCaffrey, *Elizabeth I*, London, 1993. A new biography of Elizabeth's leading adviser by Michael A. R. Graves, *Burghley: William Cecil, Lord Burghley*, Harlow, 1998, also sheds much light on the political history of the reign.

On the workings of government, David Loades, *Power in Tudor England*, London, 1997, and Penry Williams, *The Tudor regime*, Oxford, 1979, are both valuable; while political culture is very well explored in Dale Hoak (ed.), *Tudor political culture*, Cambridge, 1995. The best introductions to the extensive literature on Elizabethan parliaments are Michael A. R. Graves, *Elizabethan parliaments, 1559–1601*, 2nd edition, Harlow, 1996, and T. E. Hartley, *Elizabeth's parliaments: queen, Lords and Commons, 1559–1601*, Manchester, 1992. Finally, two collections contain several essays that relate to the themes of this book: Christopher Haigh (ed.), *The reign of Elizabeth I*, London, 1985, and John Guy (ed.), *The reign of Elizabeth I: court and culture in the last decade*, Cambridge, 1995.

The early Stuarts

A helpful overview of the political history of these years can be found in Roger Lockyer, *The early Stuarts: a political history of England, 1603–1642*, 2nd edition, Harlow, 1999. There are good surveys of James I's reign in Christopher Durston, *James I*, London, 1993; S. J. Houston, *James I*, 2nd edition, Harlow, 1995; and Roger Lockyer, *James VI and I*, Harlow, 1998. For Charles I's reign, see Christopher Durston, *Charles I*, London, 1998; Brian Quintrell, *Charles I, 1625–1640*, Harlow, 1993; and Michael B. Young, *Charles I*, London, 1997.

For contrasting interpretations of parliamentary history in this period, see Conrad Russell, *Parliaments and English politics, 1621–1629*, Oxford, 1979; and Richard Cust and Ann Hughes (eds.), *Conflict in early Stuart England: studies in religion and politics, 1603–1642*, Harlow, 1989.

On ideas of royal authority, and the limitations upon it, three particularly helpful and complementary treatments are J. P. Sommerville, *Royalists and patriots: politics and ideology in England, 1603–1640*, 2nd edition, Harlow, 1999; Glenn Burgess, *The politics of the ancient Constitution: an introduction to English political thought, 1603–1642*, London, 1992; and Glenn Burgess, *Absolute monarchy and the Stuart constitution*, New Haven and London, 1996.

The Civil Wars and Interregnum

The literature on this period is particularly voluminous. Good brief surveys are Peter Gaunt, *The British wars, 1637–1651*, London, 1997; and Martyn Bennett, *The Civil Wars in Britain and Ireland, 1638–1651*, Oxford, 1997. Also useful is G. E. Aylmer, *Rebellion or revolution? England, 1640–1660*, Oxford, 1986.

The impact of the Civil Wars on government is examined in John Morrill, *Revolt in the provinces: the people of England and the tragedies of war, 1630–1648*, 2nd edition, Harlow, 1999; John Morrill (ed.), *The impact of the English Civil War*, London, 1991; and John Morrill (ed.), *Reactions to the English Civil War, 1642–1649*, London, 1982. The effects of the conflict on ideas of royal powers, and the limitations on them, are explored in Andrew Sharp, *Political ideas of the English Civil Wars, 1641–1649*, Harlow, 1983; D. E. Kennedy, *The English revolution, 1642–1649*, London, 2000; and David L. Smith, *Constitutional royalism and the search for settlement, c. 1642–1649*, Cambridge, 1994.

On the English republic, there are good introductions in Austin Woolrych, *England without a king*, London, 1983; Toby Barnard, *The English republic*, Harlow, 1982; and Ronald Hutton, *The British republic, 1649–1660*, 2nd edition, London, 2000. John Morrill (ed.), *Revolution and Restoration: England in the 1650s*, London, 1992, contains some interesting essays on various aspects of the Interregnum. For complementary (but not always complimentary) accounts of Oliver Cromwell and his legacy, see especially Barry Coward, *Oliver Cromwell*, Harlow, 1991; Peter Gaunt, *Oliver Cromwell*, Oxford, 1996; John Morrill (ed.), *Oliver Cromwell and the English revolution*, Harlow, 1990; and David L. Smith, *Oliver Cromwell: politics and religion in the English revolution, 1640–1658*, Cambridge, 1991.

The later Stuarts

In addition to the general works listed above, an excellent overview of this period is found in Geoffrey Holmes, *The making of a great power: late Stuart and early Georgian Britain, 1660–1722*, Harlow, 1993. Also very helpful are Paul Seaward, *The Restoration, 1660–1688*, London, 1991; Tim Harris, *Politics under the later Stuarts: party conflict in a divided society, 1660–1715*, London, 1993; and Lionel K. J. Glassey (ed.), *The reigns of Charles II and James VII and II*, London, 1997. The finest biographies of Charles II are Ronald Hutton, *Charles II: king of England, Scotland and Ireland*, Oxford, 1989; and John Miller, *Charles II*, 2nd edition, London, 2000.

John Miller, *Restoration England: the reign of Charles II*, Harlow, 1985, is a good starting-point for Charles II's reign. For James II and the revolution of 1688–89, see in particular John Miller, *The Glorious Revolution*, Harlow, 1983; Michael Mullett, *James II and English politics, 1678–1688*, London, 1984; and W. A. Speck, *Reluctant revolutionaries: Englishmen and the revolution of 1688*, Oxford, 1988. A range of perspectives on the revolution itself, and the settlement that followed it, can be found in Jonathan Israel (ed.), *The Anglo-Dutch moment: essays on the Glorious Revolution and its world impact*, Cambridge, 1991; Robert Beddard (ed.), *The revolutions of 1688*, Oxford, 1991; and Lois G. Schwoerer (ed.), *The revolution of 1688–1689*, Cambridge, 1992. The most accessible accounts of the decade after the revolution can be found in Craig Rose, *England in the 1690s*, Oxford, 1999; and Julian Hoppit, *A land of liberty? England, 1689–1727*, Oxford, 2000.

Chronology

Note that the dates given for the sitting of parliaments are from their first sitting until their dissolution.

1558 *17 November:* Elizabeth succeeds to the throne

1559 *23 January–8 May: one session* First Elizabethan Parliament
Act of Uniformity levies a fine on those who refuse to attend the services of the established church
April: Peace of Cateau-Cambrésis; France and Spain make peace

1563–67 *11 January 1563–2 January 1567: two sessions* Second Elizabethan Parliament

1563 Parliament submits petitions to Elizabeth arguing that it is her duty to God to marry and settle the succession

1566 Paul Wentworth raises the issue of freedom of speech in the Commons

1567 *29 July:* James is crowned as king of Scotland

1568 Mary Queen of Scots abdicates and flees to England

1569 Rising of the northern earls

1570 Papal bull excommunicates Elizabeth

1571 *2 April–29 May: one session* Third Elizabethan Parliament
Ridolfi Plot; a plan to invade England on behalf of Mary
William Strickland promotes a bill allowing Protestant ministers to deviate from the Prayer Book

1572–83 *8 May 1572–19 April 1583: three sessions* Fourth Elizabethan Parliament

1572 Puritans submit *Admonitions to the Parliament*

1576 Peter Wentworth raises the issue of freedom of speech in the Commons

1583 Death of Edmund Grindal, archbishop of Canterbury since 1576; the anti-Puritan John Whitgift is nominated as his successor
Throckmorton Plot uncovered – a plan to encourage a foreign invasion of England, assassinate Elizabeth and place Mary upon the throne by force

1584–85 *23 November 1584–14 September 1585: one session* Fifth Elizabethan Parliament

1584 *July:* William of Orange assassinated

1585 Treaty of Nonsuch; Elizabeth commits England to assisting the Dutch against Spain – England at war with Spain until 1604

1586 Babington Plot; a scheme to place Mary on the English throne with foreign support

1586–87 *29 October 1586–23 March 1587: one session* Sixth Elizabethan Parliament

1587 *8 February:* Mary executed
27 February: Anthony Cope (MP) introduces a bill for a presbyterian form of church government

March: Peter Wentworth imprisoned on the orders of the queen and privy council whilst parliament is still sitting

1589   *4 February–29 March: one session* Seventh Elizabethan Parliament

1593   *19 February–10 April: one session* Eighth Elizabethan Parliament

1594–97   Four worst harvests of the whole of the sixteenth century

1597–98   *24 October 1597–9 February 1598: one session* Ninth Elizabethan Parliament

1601   *25 February:* Essex executed
        27 October–19 December 1601: one session Tenth Elizabethan Parliament

1603   *24 March:* Death of Elizabeth; James VI of Scotland becomes James I of England

1604   *January:* James meets with puritan representatives at Hampton Court Palace

1604–11   *19 March 1604–9 February 1611: five sessions* First Jacobean Parliament

1604   Goodwin–Fortescue election dispute
        A committee of the Commons draws up the Form of Apology and Satisfaction
        New set of Canons issued

1604–7   Debates take place in parliament about union with Scotland

1605   The Gunpowder Plot

1606   Bate's Case; James obtains judicial backing to levy impositions
        Oath of Allegiance imposed upon the Catholics

1610   Failure of the Great Contract

1611   George Abbot nominated as archbishop of Canterbury; replaces Richard Bancroft (1604–10)

1614   *5 April–7 June: one session* Second Jacobean Parliament (the Addled Parliament)

1615   Buckingham replaces Somerset as the royal favourite

1617   James visits Scotland

1618   Outbreak of the Thirty Years' War
        James publishes the Book of Sports

1621–22   *30 January 1621–6 January 1622: two sessions* Third Jacobean Parliament

1621   Commons revives impeachment; used against monopolists Michell and Mompesson and the lord chancellor, Sir Francis Bacon
        James arrests Southampton, Sandys and Oxford during the parliamentary recess
        Parliament is brought to an end with arguments over free speech, recorded in the Protestation

1624–25   *12 February 1624–27 March 1625: one session* Fourth Jacobean Parliament

1624   Commons impeach Lord Treasurer Middlesex, attach appropriation clause to their grants of subsidies and obtain the royal assent to the Monopolies Bill
        Richard Montagu publishes his *A new gag for an old goose*

1625   *27 March:* Death of James and accession of Charles I

1625   *18 June–12 August: one session* First Caroline Parliament

1625   Charles marries Henrietta Maria
        Parliament votes tonnage and poundage for only one year
        Montagu publishes *Appello Caesarem*

1625–26 Series of foreign policy disasters leads to war against France and Spain until 1629 and 1630 respectively

1626 *6 February–15 June: one session* Second Caroline Parliament
February: York House Conference; Buckingham attaches himself to the anti-Calvinists
Charles arrests several MPs whilst parliament is sitting

1627 Charles raises the Forced Loan

1628–29 *17 March 1628–10 March 1629: two sessions* Third Caroline Parliament

1628 Petition of Right
23 August: Buckingham is assassinated

1629 Commons passes the Three Resolutions

1640 *13 April–5 May: one session* Fourth Caroline Parliament (the Short Parliament)
New Canons published, including the 'Etc. Oath'

1640–53 *3 November 1640–20 April 1653* Fifth Caroline Parliament (the Long Parliament)

1641 MPs obtain the king's assent to a number of bills, including the Triennial Bill and Bill Against Forcible Dissolution, designed to restrain the royal prerogative
October: Irish rebellion
22–23 November: Grand Remonstrance passes in the Commons by only 11 votes (159 to 148)

1642 *4 January:* Charles enters the Commons intending to arrest the 'Five Members'
February: Bishops excluded from the Lords

1642–46 First Civil War

1644 Royalist parliament meets in Oxford

1646 *October:* Episcopacy abolished

1648 Second Civil War
6 December: The army purges the Long Parliament of those MPs intent upon negotiating a settlement with the king, thus creating what is known as the Rump Parliament

1649 *4 January:* Commons' resolution 'that whatsoever is enacted and declared for law by the Commons . . . has the force of law' without the consent of the king and Lords
30 January: Execution of Charles I; formation of Commonwealth government
March: Abolition of House of Lords and monarchy

1653 *20 April:* Rump Parliament is dissolved by Cromwell
4 July–12 December: Nominated Assembly
16 December: Cromwell is installed as lord protector according to the terms of the Instrument of Government

1654 Cromwell issues 82 ordinances, including those setting up the Triers and Ejectors

1654–55 *3 September 1654–22 January 1655: one session* First Protectorate Parliament; MPs question the legitimacy of the Instrument

1656–58 *17 September 1656–4 February 1658: two sessions* Second Protectorate Parliament

1656 *December:* MPs order the punishment of the Quaker James Nayler

1657 *26 June:* Cromwell is reinstalled as lord protector according to the terms of the Humble Petition and Advice

1658 *3 September:* Death of Oliver Cromwell; he is succeeded by his eldest son, Richard

1659 *27 January–22 April: one session* Third Protectorate Parliament

1659–60 *7 May–13 October and 26 December 1659–16 March 1660:* Government is undertaken by the restored Rump of the Long Parliament

1660 *25 April–29 December: two sessions* The Convention Parliament
8 May: Parliament declares Charles II to have been king since 30 January 1649
29 May: Charles II enters London
25 October: Charles issues Worcester House Declaration

1661 *January:* Fifth monarchist rebellion led by Thomas Venner

1661–79 *8 May 1661–24 January 1679: 18 sessions* The Cavalier Parliament

1661–65 A number of acts, known collectively as the 'Clarendon Code', are passed against the dissenters

1662 *20 May:* Charles marries Catherine of Braganza; the marriage is barren
26 December: Charles issues his first Declaration of Indulgence

1664 A new Triennial Act considerably dilutes the terms of the 1641 act

1670 *March:* Second Conventicle Act
May: Secret Treaty of Dover

1672 *March:* Charles issues second Declaration of Indulgence

1673 *February:* Commons votes against royal suspending power in ecclesiastical matters
March: First Test Act
June: James, duke of York, resigns as lord admiral according to the terms of the first Test Act

1678 *November:* Second Test Act

1679 *6 March–12 July: one session* First Exclusion Parliament

1680–81 *21 October 1680–18 January 1681: one session* Second Exclusion Parliament

1681 *21–28 March: one session* Third Exclusion Parliament

1684 *March:* Charles fails to call a parliament, thereby violating the Triennial Act of 1664

1685 *6 February:* Death of Charles II and accession of James II
19 May–20 November: two sessions Only Parliament of James II; not dissolved until 2 July 1687

1686 *16 June:* Godden versus Hales; judges uphold king's dispensing power
July: James establishes Commission for Ecclesiastical Causes

1687 *April:* James issues Declaration of Indulgence
October: Commission for Ecclesiastical Causes deprives fellows of Magdalen College, Oxford; James begins preparations for a packed parliament

1688 *May:* James instructs clergy to read Declaration of Indulgence from their pulpits
10 June: James's second wife, Mary of Modena, gives birth to a son
29–30 June: Archbishop Sancroft and six other bishops are acquitted after claiming that James's use of suspending power is illegal
30 June: The 'Immortal Seven' write a letter to William of Orange, inviting him to invade
5 November: William lands at Torbay
23 December: James flees to France

1689–90 *22 January 1689–6 February 1690: two sessions* The Convention Parliament

Index

Printed in the United States
By Bookmasters